Italian

Guaranteed to get you talking

D1009588

Contents

≡ Special Features

5 Phrases
To Learn Before You Go 6

10 Phrases
To Start a Sentence 8

10 Phrases
To Sound Like a Local 7

10 Phrases
To Get You Talking 96

Before You Go

You can get by in Italy's major cities without speaking Italian, but just a few phrases will go a long way in making friends, inviting service with a smile, and ensuring a rich and rewarding travel experience – you could experience a delicious meal at a no-menu trattoria, find a hidden art gallery off the tourist trail, or discover the best cappuccino in Rome.

PRONUNCIATION TIPS

The sounds of Italian can almost all be found in English, and if you read our coloured pronunciation guides as if they were English you'll be understood. The stressed syllables are indicated with italics.

★ The only sound that does differ from English is the r, which is rolled and stronger than in English.

★ Most other consonants can have a more emphatic pronunciation too (in which case they're written as double letters). The actual sounds are basically the same, but the more emphatic pronunciation can alter the meaning of a word, eg *sono* so·no means 'I am', but *sonno* son·no means 'sleep'.

★ Note also that dz is pronounced as the 'ds' in 'lids' and ly as the 'li' in 'million'.

MUST-KNOW GRAMMAR

The structure of Italian holds no major surprises for English speakers since the two languages are quite closely related.

★ Italian has a formal and informal word for 'you' (*Lei* lay and *tu* too respectively). When talking to someone familiar or younger than you, use the informal *tu* form. Phrases in this book use the form that is appropriate to the situation. Where both forms can be used, they are indicated by pol and inf respectively.

★ Italian also distinguishes between masculine and feminine forms of words, eg *bello/bella* be·lo/be·la (beautiful), indicated in this book by m and f.

★ Verbs have a different ending for each person, like the English 'I do' vs 'he/she do**es**'. Travellers don't need to worry too much about this though – if you use the dictionary form of a verb in all contexts, you'll still be understood.

SOUNDS FAMILIAR?

Numerous Italian words are already part of the English vocabulary – most of us are familiar with *ciao, pasta, bella, maestro, mafia...*

Fast Talk Italian

Don't worry if you've never learnt Italian (*italiano* ee·ta·lya·no) before – it's all about confidence. You don't need to memorise endless grammatical details or long lists of vocabulary – you just need to start speaking. You have nothing to lose and everything to gain when the locals hear you making an effort. And remember that body language and a sense of humour have a role to play in every culture.

"you just need to start speaking"

Even if you use the very basics, such as greetings and civilities, your travel experience will be the better for it. Once you start, you'll be amazed how many prompts you'll get to help you build on those first words. You'll hear people speaking, pick up sounds and expressions from the locals, catch a word or two that you know from TV already, see something on a billboard – all these things help to build your understanding.

5. Phrases to Learn Before You Go

1. What's the local speciality?
Qual'è la specialità di questa regione?
kwa·*le* la spe·cha·lee·*ta* dee *kwes*·ta re·*jo*·ne

A bit like the rivalry between medieval Italian city-states, these days the country's regions compete in specialty foods and wines

2. Which combined tickets do you have?
Quali biglietti cumulativi avete?
kwa·lee bee·*lye*·tee koo·moo·la·*tee*·vee a·*ve*·te

Make the most of your euro by getting combined tickets to various sights. They are available in all major Italian cities.

3. Where can I buy discount designer items?
C'è un outlet in zona? che oon *owt*·let in *zo*·na

Discount fashion outlets are big business in major cities – get bargain-priced seconds, samples and cast-offs for *la bella figura*.

4. I'm here with my husband/boyfriend.
Sono qui con il mio marito/ragazzo.
so·no kwee kon eel *mee*·o ma·*ree*·to/ra·*ga*·tso

Solo women travellers may receive unwanted attention in some parts of Italy. If ignoring fails, have a polite rejection ready.

5. Let's meet at 6pm for pre-dinner drinks.
Ci vediamo alle 6 per un aperitivo.
chee ve·*dya*·mo a·le say per oon a·pe·ree·*tee*·vo

At dusk, watch the main *piazza* get crowded with people sipping colourful cocktails and snacking the evening away: join your new friends for this authentic Italian ritual!

10. Phrases to Sound Like a Local

What's up? **Cosa c'è?** ko·za che

All OK? **Tutto a posto?** too·ta pos·to

It's OK. **Va bene.** va be·ne

Great! **Fantastico!** fan·tas·tee·ko

That's true. **È vero.** e ve·ro

Sure. **Certo.** cher·to

No way! **Per niente!** per nyen·te

You're kidding! **Scherzi!** sker·tsee

If only! **Magari!** ma·ga·ree

Really? **Davvero?** da·ve·ro

10. Phrases to Start a Sentence

When's (the next flight)?	A che ora è (il prossimo volo)? a ke o·ra e (eel pro·see·mo vo·lo)
Where's (the station)?	Dov'è (la stazione)? do·ve (la sta·tsyo·ne)
I'm looking for (a hotel).	Sto cercando (un albergo). sto cher·kan·do (oon al·ber·go)
Do you have (a map)?	Ha (una pianta)? a (oo·na pyan·ta)
Is there (a toilet)?	C'è (un gabinetto)? che (oon ga·bee·ne·to)
I'd like (a coffee).	Vorrei (un caffè). vo·ray (oon ka·fe)
I'd like to (hire a car).	Vorrei (noleggiare una macchina). vo·ray (no·le·ja·re oo·na ma·kee·na)
Can I (enter)?	Posso (entrare)? po·so (en·tra·re)
Can you please (help me)?	Può (aiutarmi), per favore? pwo (a·yoo·tar·mee) per fa·vo·re
Do I have to (book a seat)?	Devo (prenotare un posto)? de·vo (pre·no·ta·re oon po·sto)

Chatting & Basics

≈ Fast Phrases

Hello./Goodbye.	Buongiorno./ Arrivederci. bwon·*jor*·no/ a·ree·ve·*der*·chee
Please./Thank you.	Per favore./Grazie. per fa·*vo*·re/*gra*·tsye
Do you speak English?	Parla/Parli inglese? pol/inf *par*·la/*par*·lee een·*gle*·ze

Essentials

Yes./No.	Sì./No. see/no
Please.	Per favore. per fa·*vo*·re
Thank you (very much).	Grazie (mille). *gra*·tsye (*mee*·le)
You're welcome.	Prego. *pre*·go
Excuse me. (for attention/apology)	Mi scusi. pol mee *skoo*·zee Scusami. inf *skoo*·za·mee

Excuse me. (if going past)	Permesso. per·*me*·so
Sorry.	Mi dispiace. mee dees·*pya*·che

Language Difficulties

Do you speak English?	Parla/Parli inglese? pol/inf *par*·la/*par*·lee een·*gle*·ze
Does anyone speak English?	C'è qualcuno che parla inglese? che kwal·*koo*·no ke *par*·la een·*gle*·ze
Do you understand?	Capisce? pol ka·*pee*·she Capisci? inf ka·*pee*·shee
I (don't) understand.	(Non) Capisco. (non) ka·*pee*·sko
I speak a little.	Parlo un po'. *par*·lo oon po
What does ... mean?	Che cosa vuol dire ...? ke *ko*·za vwol *dee*·re ...
How do you pronounce this?	Come si pronuncia questo? *ko*·me see pro·*noon*·cha *kwe*·sto
How do you write ...?	Come si scrive ...? *ko*·me see *skree*·ve ...
Could you please repeat that?	Può/Puoi ripeterlo, per favore? pol/inf pwo/pwoy ree·*pe*·ter·lo per fa·*vo*·re

Could you please write it down?	Può/Puoi scriverlo, per favore? pol/inf pwo/pwoy *skree*·ver·lo per fa·*vo*·re
Could you please speak more slowly?	Può/Puoi parlare più lentamente, per favore? pol/inf pwo/pwoy par·*la*·re pyoo len·ta·*men*·te per fa·*vo*·re
✄ **Slowly, please!**	Più lentamente, per favore! pyoo len·ta·*men*·te per fa·*vo*·re

Greetings

Hello.	Buongiorno./Salve. bwon·*jor*·no/*sal*·ve
Hi.	Ciao. chow
Good morning/afternoon.	Buongiorno. bwon·*jor*·no
Good evening.	Buonasera. bwo·na·*se*·ra
Good night.	Buonanotte. bwo·na·*no*·te
See you later.	A più tardi. a pyoo *tar*·dee

Fast Talk **Greetings**

Although *ciao* chow is a common greeting, it's best not to use it when addressing strangers. Also note that in Italy the word *buonasera* bwo·na·*se*·ra (good evening) may be heard any time from early afternoon onwards.

Goodbye.	Arrivederci. a·ree·ve·*der*·chee
Bye.	Ciao. chow
How are you?	Come sta/stai? pol/inf *ko*·me sta/stai
Fine. And you?	Bene. E Lei/tu? pol/inf *be*·ne e lay/too

Titles

Mr	Signore see·*nyo*·re
Mrs	Signora see·*nyo*·ra
Miss/Ms	Signorina see·nyo·*ree*·na

Introductions

What's your name?	Come si chiama? pol *ko*·me see *kya*·ma Come ti chiami? inf *ko*·me tee *kya*·mee
My name is ...	Mi chiamo ... mee *kya*·mo ...
I'm pleased to meet you.	Piacere. pya·*che*·re
It's been great meeting you.	È stato veramente un piacere conoscerti. e *sta*·to ve·ra·*men*·te oon pya·*che*·re ko·*no*·sher·tee

I'd like to introduce you to ...	Le/Ti presento ... **pol/inf**
	le/tee pre·*zen*·to ...

This is ...	Questo/Questa è... **m/f**
	kwe·sto/kwes·ta e ...

PHRASE BUILDER

This is my ...	Le/Ti presento ... **pol/inf**	le/tee pre·*zen*·to ...
colleague	il mio collega **m**	eel *mee*·o ko·*le*·ga
	la mia collega **f**	la *mee*·a ko·*le*·ga
friend	il mio amico **m**	eel *mee*·o a·*mee*·ko
	la mia amica **f**	la *mee*·a a·*mee*·ka
husband	mio marito	*mee*·o ma·*ree*·to
partner	il mio compagno **m**	eel *mee*·o kom·*pa*·nyo
	la mia compagna **f**	la *mee*·a kom·*pa*·nya
wife	mia moglie	*mee*·a mo·lye

What's your ...?	Qual'è il Suo/tuo ...? **pol/inf**
	kwa·*le* eel *soo*·o/*too*·o ...

PHRASE BUILDER

Here's my ...	Ecco il mio ...	*e*·ko eel *mee*·o ...
address	indirizzo	een·dee·*ree*·tso
email address	indirizzo di email	een·dee·*ree*·tso dee e·mayl
mobile number	numero di cellulare	*noo*·me·ro dee che·loo·*la*·re
phone number	numero di telefono	*noo*·me·ro dee te·*le*·fo·no

Personal Details

Where are you from?	Da dove viene/vieni? **pol/inf**
	da *do*·ve *vye*·ne/*vye*·nee

PHRASE BUILDER

I'm from ...	Vengo ...	*ven*·go ...
Australia	dall'Australia	dal·ow·*stra*·lya
Canada	dal Canada	dal *ka*·na·da
England	dall'Inghilterra	da·leen·geel·*te*·ra
New Zealand	dalla Nuova Zelanda	*da*·la *nwo*·va ze·*lan*·da
the USA	dagli Stati Uniti	*da*·lyee *sta*·tee oo·*nee*·tee

Are you married?	È sposato/a? **m/f pol**
	e spo·*za*·to/a
	Sei sposato/a? **m/f inf**
	say spo·*za*·to/a
I'm single.	Sono celibe/nubile. **m/f**
	so·no *che*·lee·be/*noo*·bee·le
I'm married.	Sono sposato/a. **m/f**
	so·no spo·*za*·to/a
I'm separated.	Sono separato/a. **m/f**
	so·no se·pa·*ra*·to/a

Age

How old are you?	Quanti anni ha/hai? **pol/inf**
	kwan·tee *a*·nee a/ai
I'm ... years old.	Ho ... anni.
	o ... *a*·nee

How old is your son?	Quanti anni ha Suo/tuo figlio? pol/inf *kwan*·tee *a*·nee a *soo*·o/*too*·o *fee*·lyo
How old is your daughter?	Quanti anni ha Sua/tua figlia? pol/inf *kwan*·tee *a*·nee a *soo*·a/*too*·a *fee*·lya
He/She is ... years old.	Ha ... anni. a ... *a*·nee

Occupations & Study

What's your occupation?	Che lavoro fa/fai? pol/inf ke la·*vo*·ro fa/fai
I'm an office worker.	Sono impiegato/a. m/f *so*·no eem·pye·*ga*·to/a
I work in (administration).	Lavoro nel campo (dell'amministrazione). la·*vo*·ro nel *kam*·po (de·la·mee·nee·stra·*tsyo*·ne)
I'm retired.	Sono pensionato/a. m/f *so*·no pen·syo·*na*·to/a
I'm unemployed.	Sono disoccupato/a. m/f *so*·no dee·zo·koo·*pa*·to/a
I'm self-employed.	Lavoro in proprio. la·*vo*·ro een *pro*·pryo
I'm a student.	Sono studente. m *so*·no stoo·*den*·te Sono studentessa. f *so*·no stoo·den·*te*·sa
What are you studying?	Cosa studia/studi? pol/inf *ko*·za *stoo*·dya/*stoo*·dee

| I'm studying engineering. | Sto studiando ingegneria. sto stoo·*dyan*·do een·je·nye·*ree*·a |
| I'm studying humanities. | Sto studiando lettere. sto stoo·*dyan*·do *le*·te·re |

Interests

| What do you do in your spare time? | Cosa fai nel tuo tempo libero? *ko*·za fai nel *too*·o *tem*·po *lee*·be·ro |
| Do you like ...? | Ti piace/piacciono ...? sg/pl tee *pya*·che/*pya*·cho·no ... |

PHRASE BUILDER

I (don't) like ...	(Non) Mi piace/ piacciono ... sg/pl	(non) mee *pya*·che/ *pya*·cho·no ...
art	l'arte sg	*lar*·te
cooking	cucinare sg	koo·chee·*na*·re
film	i film pl	ee feelm
music	la musica sg	la *moo*·zee·ka
sport	lo sport sg	lo sport

Feelings

Are you (sad)?	È/Sei (triste)? pol/inf e/say (*tree*·ste)
I'm (tired).	Sono (stanco/a). m/f *so*·no (*stan*·ko/a)
I'm not (happy).	Non sono (felice). non *so*·no (fe·*lee*·che)

Are you ...?	Ha/Hai ...? pol/inf
	a/ai ...

PHRASE BUILDER

I'm (not) ...	(Non) Ho ...	(non) o ...
cold	freddo	*fre*·do
hot	caldo	*kal*·do
hungry	fame	*fa*·me
in a hurry	fretta	*fre*·ta
thirsty	sete	*se*·te

Numbers

1	uno	*oo*·no
2	due	*doo*·e
3	tre	tre
4	quattro	*kwa*·tro
5	cinque	*cheen*·kwe
6	sei	say
7	sette	*se*·te
8	otto	*o*·to
9	nove	*no*·ve
10	dieci	*dye*·chee
11	undici	*oon*·dee·chee
12	dodici	*do*·dee·chee
13	tredici	*tre*·dee·chee
14	quattordici	kwa·*tor*·dee·chee
15	quindici	*kween*·dee·chee
16	sedici	*se*·dee·chee

17	diciassette	dee·cha·se·te
18	diciotto	dee·cho·to
19	diciannove	dee·cha·no·ve
20	venti	ven·tee
21	ventuno	ven·too·no
30	trenta	tren·ta
40	quaranta	kwa·ran·ta
50	cinquanta	cheen·kwan·ta
60	sessanta	se·san·ta
70	settanta	se·tan·ta
80	ottanta	o·tan·ta
90	novanta	no·van·ta
100	cento	chen·to
1000	mille	mee·le
1,000,000	un milione	oon mee·lyo·ne

Time

What time is it?	Che ora è?	ke o·ra e
It's one o'clock.	È l'una.	e loo·na
It's (two) o'clock.	Sono le (due).	so·no le (doo·e)
Quarter past (one).	(L'una) e un quarto.	(loo·na) e oon kwar·to
Half past (one).	(L'una) e mezza.	(loo·na) e me·dza
Quarter to (eight).	(Le otto) meno un quarto.	(le o·to) me·no oon kwar·to

Fast Talk — Telling the Time

The 24-hour clock is commonly used when telling the time in Italian. 'It is ...' is expressed by *Sono le ...* *so*·no le ..., followed by a number – but 'one o'clock' is *È l'una* e *loo*·na. For times up to the half hour use *e* e (and). For times after the half hour, say the next hour 'minus' (*meno* me·no) the minutes until that hour arrives, eg 'twenty to eight' is *le otto meno venti* le *o*·to *me*·no *ven*·tee (lit: eight minus twenty).

At what time ...?	A che ora ...? a ke *o*·ra ...
At (six).	Alle (sei). a·le (say)
in the morning	di mattina dee ma·*tee*·na
in the afternoon	di pomeriggio dee po·me·*ree*·jo
in the evening	di sera dee *se*·ra

Days

Monday	lunedì m	loo·ne·*dee*
Tuesday	martedì m	mar·te·*dee*
Wednesday	mercoledì m	mer·ko·*le*·dee
Thursday	giovedì m	jo·ve·*dee*
Friday	venerdì m	ve·ner·*dee*
Saturday	sabato m	*sa*·ba·to
Sunday	domenica f	do·*me*·nee·ka

Months

January	gennaio m	je·na·yo
February	febbraio m	fe·bra·yo
March	marzo m	mar·tso
April	aprile m	a·pree·le
May	maggio m	ma·jo
June	giugno m	joo·nyo
July	luglio m	loo·lyo
August	agosto m	a·gos·to
September	settembre m	se·tem·bre
October	ottobre m	o·to·bre
November	novembre m	no·vem·bre
December	dicembre m	dee·chem·bre

Dates

What date is it today?	Che giorno è oggi?
	ke jor·no e o·jee
It's (3 March).	È (il terzo) marzo.
	e (eel ter·tso mar·tso)
yesterday morning	ieri mattina
	ye·ree ma·tee·na
tomorrow morning	domani mattina
	do·ma·nee ma·tee·na
yesterday afternoon	ieri pomeriggio
	ye·ree po·me·ree·jo
tomorrow afternoon	domani pomeriggio
	do·ma·nee po·me·ree·jo
yesterday evening	ieri sera
	ye·ree se·ra

Fast Talk **Starting Off**

When starting to speak another language, your biggest hurdle is saying aloud what may seem to be just a bunch of sounds. The best way to do this is to memorise a few key words, like 'hello', 'thank you' and 'how much?', plus at least one phrase that's not essential, eg 'how are you', 'see you later' or 'it's very cold/hot' (people love to talk about the weather!). This will enable you to make contact with the locals, and when you get a reply and a smile, it'll also boost your confidence.

tomorrow evening	domani sera do·*ma*·nee *se*·ra
last week	la settimana scorsa la se·tee·*ma*·na *skor*·sa
next week	la settimana prossima la se·tee·*ma*·na *pro*·see·ma
last month	il mese scorso eel *me*·ze *skor*·so
next month	il mese prossimo eel *me*·ze *pro*·see·mo
last year	l'anno scorso *la*·no *skor*·so
next year	l'anno prossimo *la*·no *pro*·see·mo

Weather

What's the weather forecast?	Cosa dicono le previsioni del tempo? *ko*·za *dee*·ko·no le pre·vee·*zyo*·nee del *tem*·po

21

Fast Talk **Negatives**

To make a negative statement in Italian, just add the word *non* non (not) before the main verb of the sentence. Unlike English, Italian uses double negatives, eg *non capisco niente* non ka·*pee*·sko *nyen*·te (lit: not I-understand nothing) means 'I don't understand anything'.

What's the weather like?	Che tempo fa? ke *tem*·po fa
It's (very) cold.	Fa (molto) freddo. fa (*mol*·to) *fre*·do
It's hot.	Fa caldo. fa *kal*·do
It's raining.	Piove. *pyo*·ve
It's snowing.	Nevica. ne·*vee*·ka
It's sunny.	È soleggiato. e so·le·*ja*·to
It's windy.	Tira vento. *tee*·ra *ven*·to

Directions

Where's (the bank)?	Dov'è (la banca)? do·*ve* (la *ban*·ka)
Which way is (the post office)?	Dove si trova (l'ufficio postale)? *do*·ve see *tro*·va (loo·*fee*·cho pos·*ta*·le)

What's the address?	Qual'è l'indirizzo? kwa·*le* leen·dee·*ree*·tso
Could you please write it down?	Può/Puoi scriverlo, per favore? pol/inf pwo/pwoy *skree*·ver·lo per fa·*vo*·re
Can you show me (on the map)?	Può mostrarmi (sulla pianta)? pwo mos·*trar*·mee (*soo*·la *pyan*·ta)
How far is it?	Quant'è distante? kwan·*te* dees·*tan*·te
Turn at the corner.	Giri all'angolo. *jee*·ree a·*lan*·go·lo
Turn at the traffic lights.	Giri al semaforo. *jee*·ree al se·*ma*·fo·ro
Turn left.	Giri a sinistra. *jee*·ree a see·*nee*·stra
Turn right.	Giri a destra. *jee*·ree a *de*·stra
behind ...	dietro ... *dye*·tro ...
in front of ...	davanti a ... da·*van*·tee a ...
next to ...	accanto a ... a·*kan*·to a ...
opposite ...	di fronte a ... dee *fron*·te a ...
straight ahead	sempre diritto *sem*·pre dee·*ree*·to

Airport & Transport

Fast Phrases

When's the next (bus)?	A che ora passa il prossimo (autobus)? a ke *o*·ra *pa*·sa eel *pro*·see·mo (*ow*·to·boos)
Does this (train) stop at ...?	Questo (treno) si ferma a ...? *kwe*·sto (*tre*·no) see *fer*·ma a ...
One ticket to ..., please.	Un biglietto per ..., per favore. oon bee·*lye*·to per ..., per fa·*vo*·re

At the Airport

I'm here on business.	Sono qui per affari. *so*·no kwee per a·*fa*·ree
I'm here on holiday.	Sono qui in vacanza. *so*·no kwee een va·*kan*·tsa
I'm here for (three) days.	Sono qui per (tre) giorni. *so*·no kwee per (tre) *jor*·nee
I'm here for (two) weeks.	Sono qui per (due) settimane. *so*·no kwee per (*doo*·e) se·tee·*ma*·ne

24

I'm in transit.	Sono in transito.
	so·no een tran·see·to
I'm going to (Perugia).	Vado a (Perugia).
	va·do a (pe·roo·ja)
I have nothing to declare.	Non ho niente da dichiarare.
	non o nyen·te da dee·kya·ra·re
I have something to declare.	Ho delle cose da dichiarare.
	o de·le ko·ze da dee·kya·ra·re

Getting Around

PHRASE BUILDER

At what time does the ... leave?	A che ora parte ...?	a ke o·ra par·te ...
boat	la nave	la na·ve
bus	l'autobus	low·to·boos
plane	l'aereo	la·e·re·o
train	il treno	eel tre·no

When's the first bus?	A che ora passa il primo autobus?
	a ke o·ra pa·sa eel pree·mo ow·to·boos
When's the last bus?	A che ora passa l'ultimo autobus?
	a ke o·ra pa·sa lool·tee·mo ow·to·boos
When's the next bus?	A che ora passa il prossimo autobus?
	a ke o·ra pa·sa eel pro·see·mo ow·to·boos

How long does the trip take?	Quanto ci vuole? *kwan*·to chee *vwo*·le
Is it a direct route?	È un itinerario diretto? e oon ee·tee·ne·*ra*·ryo dee·*re*·to
That's my seat.	Quel posto è mio. kwel *pos*·to e *mee*·o
Is this seat free?	È libero questo posto? e *lee*·be·ro *kwe*·sto *pos*·to
✂ Is it free?	È libero? e *lee*·be·ro

Buying Tickets

Where can I buy a ticket?	Dove posso comprare un biglietto? *do*·ve *po*·so kom·*pra*·re oon bee·*lye*·to
Do I need to book?	Bisogna prenotare un posto? bee·*zo*·nya pre·no·*ta*·re oon *pos*·to

Fast Talk   **Asking Questions**

The easiest way of forming 'yes/no' questions in Italian is to add the phrase *è vero* e *ve*·ro (lit: is-it true) to the end of a statement, similar to 'isn't it?' in English.

The question words for more specific questions go at the start of the sentence: *come* ko·me (how), *che cosa* ke ko·za (what), *quando* kwan·do (when), *dove* do·ve (where), *chi* kee (who) or *perché* per·ke (why).

What time do I have to check in?

A che ora devo presentarmi per l'accettazione?
a ke o·ra de·vo pre·zen·tar·mee per la·che·ta·tsyo·ne

One ... ticket (to Rome), please.	Un biglietto ... (per Roma), per favore.	oon bee·lye·to ... (per ro·ma) per fa·vo·re
1st-class	di prima classe	dee pree·ma kla·se
2nd-class	di seconda classe	dee se·kon·da kla·se
child's	per bambini	per bam·bee·nee
one-way	di sola andata	dee so·la an·da·ta
return	di andata e ritorno	dee an·da·ta e ree·tor·no
student's	per studenti	per stoo·den·tee

I'd like an aisle seat, please.

Vorrei un posto sul corridoio, per favore.
vo·ray oon pos·to sool ko·ree·do·yo per fa·vo·re

I'd like a window seat, please.

Vorrei un posto vicino al finestrino, per favore.
vo·ray oon pos·to vee·chee·no al fee·nes·tree·no per fa·vo·re

I'd like a (non)smoking seat, please.

Vorrei un posto per (non) fumatori, per favore.
vo·ray oon pos·to per (non) foo·ma·to·ree per fa·vo·re

Luggage

My luggage has been damaged.	Il mio bagaglio è stato danneggiato. eel *mee*·o ba·*ga*·lyo e *sta*·to da·ne·*ja*·to
My luggage has been lost.	Il mio bagaglio è stato perso. eel *mee*·o ba·*ga*·lyo e *sta*·to *per*·so
My luggage has been stolen.	Il mio bagaglio è stato rubato. eel *mee*·o ba·*ga*·lyo e *sta*·to roo·*ba*·to
I'd like a luggage locker.	Vorrei un armadietto per il bagaglio. vo·*ray* oon ar·ma·*dye*·to per eel ba·*ga*·lyo
I'd like some coins.	Vorrei della moneta. vo·*ray* de·la mo·*ne*·ta
I'd like some tokens.	Vorrei dei gettoni. vo·*ray* day je·*to*·nee

Bus & Train

Where's the bus stop?	Dov'è la fermata dell'autobus? *do*·ve la fer·*ma*·ta del·*ow*·to·boos
Which bus goes to ...?	Quale autobus va a ...? *kwa*·le *ow*·to·boos va a ...
Is this the bus to ...?	Questo autobus va a ...? *kwe*·sto *ow*·to·boos va a ...
What station is this?	Che stazione è questa? ke sta·*tsyo*·ne e *kwe*·sta

What's the next station?	Qual'è la prossima stazione? kwa·*le* la *pro*·see·ma sta·*tsyo*·ne
What's the next stop?	Qual'è la prossima fermata? kwa·*le* la *pro*·see·ma fer·*ma*·ta
Does this train stop at ...?	Questo treno si ferma a ...? *kwe*·sto *tre*·no see *fer*·ma a ...
Do I need to change trains?	Devo cambiare treno? *de*·vo kam·*bya*·re *tre*·no
How many stops to ...?	Quante fermate mancano ...? *kwan*·te fer·*ma*·te *man*·ka·no ...
Can you tell me when we get to ...?	Mi sa dire quando arriviamo a ...? mee sa *dee*·re *kwan*·do a·ree·*vya*·mo a ...
I want to get off at ...	Voglio scendere a ... *vo*·lyo *shen*·de·re a ...
I want to get off here.	Voglio scendere qui. *vo*·lyo *shen*·de·re kwee

Taxi

Where's the taxi stand?	Dov'è la fermata dei tassì? do·*ve* la fer·*ma*·ta day ta·*see*
I'd like a taxi at (9am).	Vorrei un tassì alle (nove di mattina). vo·*ray* oon ta·*see* a·le (*no*·ve dee ma·*tee*·na)
Is this taxi free?	È libero questo tassì? e *lee*·be·ro *kwe*·sto ta·*see*
Is it free?	È libero? e *lee*·be·ro

How much is it to ...?	Quant'è per ...? kwan·*te* per ...
Please put the meter on.	Usi il tassametro, per favore. *oo*·zee eel ta·*sa*·me·tro per fa·*vo*·re
Please take me to (this address).	Mi porti a (questo indirizzo), per piacere. mee *por*·tee a (*kwe*·sto een·dee·*ree*·tso) per pya·*che*·re
✂ To ...	A ... a ...
Please slow down.	Rallenti, per favore. ra·*len*·tee per fa·*vo*·re
Please wait here.	Mi aspetti qui, per favore. mee as·*pe*·tee kwee per fa·*vo*·re
Stop at the corner.	Si fermi all'angolo. see *fer*·mee a *lan*·go·lo
Stop here.	Si fermi qui. see *fer*·mee kwee

Car & Motorbike

I'd like to hire a car.	Vorrei noleggiare una macchina. vo·*ray* no·le·*ja*·re *oo*·na *ma*·kee·na
I'd like to hire a motorbike.	Vorrei noleggiare una moto. vo·*ray* no·le·*ja*·re *oo*·na *mo*·to
How much is it daily?	Quanto costa al giorno? *kwan*·to *kos*·ta al *jor*·no

How much is it weekly?	Quanto costa alla settimana? *kwan*·to *kos*·ta *a*·la se·tee·*ma*·na
Is this the road to ...?	Questa strada porta a ...? *kwe*·sta *stra*·da *por*·ta a ...
(How long) Can I park here?	(Per quanto tempo) Posso parcheggiare qui? (per *kwan*·to *tem*·po) *po*·so par·ke·*ja*·re kwee
Where's a petrol station?	Dov'è una stazione di servizio? do·*ve* *oo*·na sta·*tsyo*·ne dee ser·*vee*·tsyo
I need a mechanic.	Ho bisogno di un meccanico. o bee·*zo*·nyo dee oon me·*ka*·nee·ko

Cycling

Where can I hire a bicycle?	Dove posso noleggiare una bicicletta? *do*·ve *po*·so no·le·*ja*·re *oo*·na bee·chee·*kle*·ta
Are there cycling paths?	Ci sono piste ciclabili? chee *so*·no *pee*·ste chee·*kla*·bee·lee
Is there bicycle parking?	C'è un posteggio per le biciclette? chay oon po·*ste*·jo per le bee·chee·*kle*·te
I have a puncture.	Ho una gomma bucata. o *oo*·na *go*·ma boo·*ka*·ta

Accommodation

≡ Fast Phrases

I have a reservation.	Ho una prenotazione. o oo·na pre·no·ta·tsyo·ne
(When/Where) is breakfast served?	(A che ora è/Dove si prende) la prima colazione? (a ke o·ra e/dove si prende) la *pree*·ma ko·la·*tsyo*·ne
What time is checkout?	A che ora si deve lasciar libera la camera? a ke o·ra see de·ve la·shar lee·be·ra la ka·me·ra

Finding Accommodation

PHRASE BUILDER

Where's a/an ...?	Dov'è ...?	do·ve ...
camping ground	un campeggio	oon kam·pe·jo
guesthouse	una pensione	oo·na pen·syo·ne
hotel	un albergo	oo·nal·ber·go
inn	una locanda	oo·na lo·kan·da
youth hostel	un ostello della gioventù	oo·nos·te·lo de·la jo·ven·too

Booking & Checking In

I have a reservation.	Ho una prenotazione. o oo·na pre·no·ta·*tsyo*·ne
Do you have a single room?	Avete una camera singola? a·*ve*·te oo·na *ka*·me·ra *seen*·go·la
Do you have a double room?	Avete una camera doppia con letto matrimoniale? a·*ve*·te oo·na *ka*·me·ra *do*·pya kon *le*·to ma·tree·mo·*nya*·le
Do you have a twin room?	Avete una camera doppia a due letti? a·*ve*·te oo·na *ka*·me·ra *do*·pya a *doo*·e *le*·tee
✂ Are there rooms?	Avete camere libere? a·*ve*·te *ka*·me·ray *lee*·be·ray
How much is it per night?	Quanto costa per una notte? *kwan*·to *kos*·ta per oo·na *no*·te
How much is it per person?	Quanto costa per persona? *kwan*·to *kos*·ta per per·*so*·na
How much is it per week?	Quanto costa per una settimana? *kwan*·to *kos*·ta per oo·na se·tee·*ma*·na
For (three) nights.	Per (tre) notti. per (tre) *no*·tee
From (July 2) to (July 6).	Dal (due luglio) al (sei luglio). dal (*doo*·e *loo*·lyo) al (say *loo*·lyo)

Hotels

Can you recommend somewhere cheap?	Può consigliare qualche posto economico? pwo kon·see·*lya*·re kwal·ke *pos*·to e·ko·*no*·mee·ko
Can you recommend somewhere nearby?	Può consigliare qualche posto vicino? pwo kon·see·*lya*·re kwal·ke *pos*·to vee·*chee*·no
Can you recommend somewhere romantic?	Può consigliare qualche posto romantico? pwo kon·see·*lya*·re kwal·ke *pos*·to ro·*man*·tee·ko

Can I see it?	Posso vederla? *po*·so ve·*der*·la
Is breakfast included?	La colazione è compresa? la ko·la·*tsyo*·ne e kom·*pre*·sa
It's fine, I'll take it.	Va bene, la prendo. va *be*·ne la *pren*·do
Do I need to pay upfront?	Devo pagare in anticipo? *de*·vo pa·*ga*·re ee·nan·*tee*·chee·po

Requests & Questions

When's breakfast served?	A che ora è la prima colazione? a ke *o*·ra e la *pree*·ma ko·la·*tsyo*·ne

Where's breakfast served?	Dove si prende la prima colazione?
	do·ve see pren·de la pree·ma ko·la·tsyo·ne
Please wake me at (seven).	Mi svegli (alle sette), per favore.
	mee sve·lyee (a·le se·te) per fa·vo·re
Can I have my key, please?	Può darmi la mia chiave, per favore?
	pwo dar·mee la mee·a kya·ve per fa·vo·re
Can I use the kitchen?	Posso usare la cucina?
	po·so oo·za·re la koo·chee·na
Can I use the telephone?	Posso usare il telefono?
	po·so oo·za·re eel te·le·fo·no
Can I use the internet?	Posso usare l'Internet?
	po·so oo·za·re leen·ter·net
Do you have an elevator?	C'è un ascensore?
	che oo·na·shen·so·re

Fast Talk Using Patterns

Look out for patterns of words or phrases that stay the same, even when the situation changes, eg 'Do you have ...?' or 'I'd like to ...' (see p8). If you can recognise these patterns, you're already halfway to creating a full phrase. The dictionary will help you put other words together with these patterns to convey your meaning – even if it's not completely grammatically correct in all contexts, the dictionary form will always be understood.

Do you have a laundry service?	C'è il servizio lavanderia? che eel ser·*vee*·tsyo la·van·de·*ree*·a
Do you have a safe?	C'è una cassaforte? che *oo*·na ka·sa·*for*·te
Do you change money here?	Si cambiano i soldi qui? see *kam*·bya·no ee *sol*·dee kwee
Do you arrange tours here?	Si organizzano le gite qui? see or·ga·*nee*·dza·no le *jee*·te kwee

Complaints

| There's no hot water. | Non c'è acqua calda. non chay *ak*·wa *kal*·da |

PHRASE BUILDER

The ... doesn't work.	... non funziona.	... non foon·*tsyo*·na
air-conditioning	L'aria condizionata	*la*·rya kon·dee·tsyo·*na*·ta
heater	La stufa	la *stoo*·fa
toilet	Il gabinetto	eel ga·bee·*ne*·to
window	La finestra	la fee·*nes*·tra

The room is too dark.	La camera è troppo scura. la *ka*·me·ra e *tro*·po *skoo*·ra
The room is too noisy.	La camera è troppo rumorosa. la *ka*·me·ra e *tro*·po roo·mo·*ro*·za
The room is too small.	La camera è troppo piccola. la *ka*·me·ra e *tro*·po *pee*·ko·la

PHRASE BUILDER

Can I get another ...?	Può darmi un altro/a ...? m/f	pwo *dar*·mee oo·*nal*·tro/a ...
blanket	coperta f	ko·*per*·ta
pillow	cuscino m	koo·*shee*·no
sheet	lenzuolo m	len·*tswo*·lo
towel	asciugamano m	a·shoo·ga·*ma*·no

Checking Out

What time is checkout?	A che ora si deve lasciar libera la camera? a ke o·*ra* see *de*·ve la·*shar* lee·*be*·ra la *ka*·me·ra
Can I leave my luggage here until (tonight)?	Posso lasciare il mio bagaglio qui fino (a stasera)? *po*·so la·*sha*·re eel *mee*·o ba·*ga*·lyo kwee *fee*·no (a sta·*se*·ra)
Can I have my deposit, please?	Posso avere la caparra, per favore? *po*·so a·*ve*·re la ka·*pa*·ra per fa·*vo*·re
Can I have my valuables, please?	Posso avere i miei oggetti di valore, per favore? *po*·so a·*ve*·re ee myay o·*je*·tee dee va·*lo*·re per fa·*vo*·re
I had a great stay, thank you.	Sono stato/a benissimo/a, grazie. m/f *so*·no *sta*·to/a be·*nee*·see·mo/a *gra*·tsye

Eating & Drinking

⇒ Fast Phrases

Can I see the menu, please?	Posso vedere il menù, per favore? *po·so ve·de·re eel me·noo per fa·vo·re*
I'd like (a beer), please.	Vorrei (una birra), per favore. *vo·ray (oo·na bee·ra) per fa·vo·re*
Please bring the bill.	Mi porta il conto, per favore? *mee por·ta eel kon·to per fa·vo·re*

Meals

breakfast	prima colazione f *pree·ma ko·la·tsyo·ne*
lunch	pranzo m *pran·dzo*
dinner	cena f *che·na*
eat/drink	mangiare/bere *man·ja·re/be·re*

Local Knowledge — Restaurants

Where would you go for a cheap meal?	Dove andrebbe per un pasto economico? *do·ve an·dre·be per oon pas·to e·ko·no·mee·ko*
Where would you go for local specialities?	Dove andrebbe per le specialità locali? *do·ve an·dre·be per le spe·cha·lee·ta lo·ka·lee*
Where would you go for a celebration?	Dove andrebbe per una celebrazione? *do·ve an·dre·be per oo·na che·le·bra·tsyo·ne*

Finding A Place to Eat

Can you recommend a bar?	Potrebbe consigliare un bar? *po·tre·be kon·see·lya·re oon bar*
Can you recommend a cafe?	Potrebbe consigliare un caffè? *po·tre·be kon·see·lya·re oon ka·fe*
Can you recommend a restaurant?	Potrebbe consigliare un ristorante? *po·tre·be kon·see·lya·re oon rees·to·ran·te*
I'd like to reserve a table for (eight) o'clock.	Vorrei prenotare un tavolo per le (otto). *vo·ray pre·no·ta·re oon ta·vo·lo per le (o·to)*

I'd like to reserve a table for (two) people.	Vorrei prenotare un tavolo per (due) persone. vo·*ray* pre·no·*ta*·re oon *ta*·vo·lo per (*doo*·e) per·*so*·ne
✂ **For two, please.**	Per due, per favore. per *doo*·e per fa·*vo*·re
I'd like a table in the (non)smoking area, please.	Vorrei un tavolo per (non) fumatori, per favore. vo·*ray* oon *ta*·vo·lo per (non) foo·ma·*to*·ree per fa·*vo*·re
Are you still serving food?	Servite ancora da mangiare? ser·*vee*·te an·*ko*·ra da man·*ja*·re
How long is the wait?	Quanto si deve aspettare? *kwan*·to see *de*·ve as·pe·*ta*·re

Ordering & Paying

Can I see the menu, please?	Posso vedere il menù, per favore? *po*·so ve·*de*·re eel me·*noo* per fa·*vo*·re
✂ **Menu, please.**	Il menù, per favore. eel me·*noo* per fa·*vo*·re
What would you recommend?	Cosa mi consiglia? *ko*·za mee kon·*see*·lya
What's the local speciality?	Qual'è la specialità di questa regione? kwa·*le* la spe·cha·lee·*ta* dee *kwe*·sta re·*jo*·ne
I'd like that one, please.	Vorrei quello/a, per favore. m/f vo·*ray* *kwe*·lo/a per fa·*vo*·re

I'd like the drink list, please.	Vorrei la lista delle bevande, per favore. vo·*ray* la *lee*·sta *de*·le be·*van*·de per fa·*vo*·re
We're just having drinks.	Prendiamo solo da bere. pren·*dya*·mo *so*·lo da *be*·re
✂ Just drinks.	Solo da bere, grazie. *so*·lo da *be*·re *gra*·tsye

PHRASE BUILDER

I'd like it ...	Lo vorrei ...	lo vo·*ray* ...
medium	non troppo cotto	non *tro*·po *ko*·to
rare	al sangue	al *san*·gwe
steamed	cotto a vapore	*ko*·to a va·*po*·re
well-done	ben cotto	ben *ko*·to
with (the dressing on the side)	con (il condimento a parte)	kon (eel kon·dee·*men*·to a *par*·te)
without ...	senza ...	*sen*·tsa ...

Please bring (a glass).	Mi porta (un bicchiere), per favore? mee *por*·ta (oon bee·*kye*·re) per fa·*vo*·re
Is there (Parmesan cheese)?	C'è (del parmigiano)? che (del par·mee·*ja*·no)
I didn't order this.	Questo non l'ho ordinato. *kwe*·sto non lo or·dee·*na*·to
This is (too) cold.	Questo è (troppo) freddo. *kwe*·sto e (*tro*·po) *fre*·do

	That was delicious!	Era squisito! *e·ra* skwee·*zee·*to
	Please bring the bill.	Mi porta il conto, per favore? mee *por*·ta eel *kon*·to per fa·*vo*·re
✂	**Bill, please.**	Il conto, per favore. eel *kon*·to per fa·*vo*·re
	There's a mistake in the bill.	C'è un errore nel conto. che oo·ne·*ro*·re nel *kon*·to

Special Diets & Allergies

Is there a vegetarian restaurant near here?	C'è un ristorante vegetariano qui vicino? che oon rees·to·*ran*·te ve·je·ta·*rya*·no kwee vee·*chee*·no
Do you have vegetarian food?	Avete piatti vegetariani? a·*ve*·te *pya*·tee ve·je·ta·*rya*·nee
I'm a vegan.	Sono vegetaliano/a. **m/f** *so*·no ve·je·ta·*lya*·no/a

Fast Talk · Practising Italian

If you want to practise your language skills, try the waiters at a restaurant. Find your feet with straight-forward phrases such as asking for a table and ordering a drink, then initiate a conversation by asking for menu recommendations or asking how a dish is cooked. And as you'll often know food terms even before you've 'officially' learnt a word of the language, you're already halfway there to understanding the response.

I'm a vegetarian.	Sono vegetariano/a. m/f *so*·no ve·je·ta·*rya*·no/a
I don't eat (red meat).	Non mangio (carne rossa). non *man*·jo (*kar*·ne *ro*·sa)
Could you prepare a meal without butter?	Potreste preparare un pasto senza burro? po·*tres*·te pre·pa·*ra*·re oon *pas*·to *sen*·tsa *boo*·ro
Could you prepare a meal without eggs?	Potreste preparare un pasto senza uova? po·*tres*·te pre·pa·*ra*·re oon *pas*·to *sen*·tsa *wo*·va
Could you prepare a meal without meat stock?	Potreste preparare un pasto senza brodo di carne? po·*tres*·te pre·pa·*ra*·re oon *pas*·to *sen*·tsa *bro*·do dee *kar*·ne

PHRASE BUILDER

I'm allergic to ...	Sono allergico/a ... m/f	*so*·no a·*ler*·jee·ko/a ...
dairy produce	ai latticini	ai la·tee·*chee*·nee
fish	al pesce	al *pe*·she
gluten	al glutine	al *gloo*·tee·ne
MSG	al glutammato monosodico	al gloo·ta·*ma*·to mo·no·so·*dee*·ko
nuts	alle noci	*a*·le *no*·chee
peanuts	alle arachidi	*a*·le a·*ra*·kee·dee
seafood	ai frutti di mare	ai *froo*·tee dee *ma*·re
shellfish	ai crostacei	ai kros·*ta*·che·ee

Nonalcoholic Drinks

coffee (without sugar)	caffè m (senza zucchero) ka·*fe* (*sen*·tsa *tsoo*·ke·ro)
orange juice	succo m d'arancia *soo*·ko da·*ran*·cha
fruit juice (bottled)	succo m di frutta *soo*·ko dee *froo*·ta
fruit juice (fresh)	spremuta f spre·*moo*·ta
soft drink	bibita f *bee*·bee·ta
tea (with milk)	tè m (con latte) te (kon *la*·te)
(mineral) water	acqua f (minerale) *a*·kwa (mee·ne·*ra*·le)

Alcoholic Drinks

a shot of ...	un sorso di ... oon *sor*·so dee ...
draught beer	birra f a la spina *bee*·ra a la *spee*·na

PHRASE BUILDER

a ... of beer	... di birra	... dee *bee*·ra
bottle	una bottiglia	*oo*·na bo·*tee*·lya
glass	un bicchiere	oon bee·*kye*·re
jug	una caraffa	*oo*·na ka·*ra*·fa
pint	una pinta	*oo*·na *peen*·ta

a bottle of ... wine	una bottiglia di vino ... *oo*·na bo·*tee*·lya dee *vee*·no ...

PHRASE BUILDER

a glass of ... wine	un bicchiere di vino ...	oon bee·*kye*·re dee *vee*·no ...
dessert	da dessert	da de·*sert*
red	rosso	*ro*·so
rose	rosato	ro·*za*·to
sparkling	spumante	spoo·*man*·te
white	bianco	*byan*·ko

In the Bar

I'll buy you a drink.	Ti offro da bere.
	tee *of*·ro da *be*·re
What would you like?	Cosa prendi?
	ko·za *pren*·dee
I'll have ...	Prendo ...
	pren·do ...
Same again, please.	Un altro, per favore.
	oon *al*·tro per fa·*vo*·re
It's my round.	Offro io.
	of·ro *ee*·o
Cheers!	Salute!
	sa·*loo*·te

Buying Food

How much is (a kilo of cheese)?	Quanto costa (un chilo di formaggio)?
	kwan·to *kos*·ta
	(oon *kee*·lo dee for·*ma*·jo)

What's that?	Cos'è?
	ko·*ze*
Do you have other kinds?	Avete altri tipi?
	a·*ve*·te *al*·tree *tee*·pee
Can I taste it?	Lo/La posso assaggiare? m/f
	lo/la *po*·so a·sa·*ja*·re

PHRASE BUILDER

I'd like ...	Vorrei ...	vo·*ray* ...
100 grams	un etto	oon e·to
200 grams	due etti	*doo*·e e·tee
(two) kilos	(due) chili	(*doo*·e) *kee*·lee
(three) pieces	(tre) pezzi	(tre) *pe*·tsee
(six) slices	(sei) fette	(say) *fe*·te
some ...	alcuni ... m	al·*koo*·nee ...
	alcune ... f	al·*koo*·ne ...
that one	quello/a m/f	*kwe*·lo/a
this one	questo/a m/f	*kwe*·sto/a

Less.	(Di) Meno.
	(dee) *me*·no
Enough.	Basta, grazie.
	bas·ta *gra*·tsye
A bit more.	Un po' di più.
	oon po dee pyoo

Menu Decoder

This miniguide to Italian cuisine is designed to help you navigate menus. Italian nouns, and adjectives affected by gender, have their gender indicated by ⓜ or ⓕ. If it's a plural noun, you'll also see pl.

- a -

acciughe ⓕ pl a·*choo*·ge anchovies
aceto ⓜ a·*che*·to vinegar
affumicato/a ⓜ/ⓕ a·foo·mee·*ka*·to/a smoked
aglio ⓜ a·lyo garlic
agnello ⓜ a·*nye*·lo lamb
al dente al *den*·te 'to the tooth' – describes cooked pasta & rice that are still slightly hard
al forno al *for*·no cooked in an oven
al sangue al *san*·gwe rare
al vapore al va·*po*·re steamed
alla diavola a·la *dya*·vo·la spiced
alla napoletana a·la na·po·le·*ta*·na from or in the style of Naples – usually includes tomatoes & garlic
all'amatriciana al·a·ma·tree·*cha*·na spicy sauce with salami, tomato, capsicums & cheese
all'arrabbiata al·a·ra·*bya*·ta 'angry-style' – with spicy sauce
antipasti ⓜ pl an·tee·*pas*·tee appetizers • hors d'oeuvres
aperitivi ⓜ pl a·pe·ree·*tee*·vee aperitifs
aragosta ⓕ a·ra·*go*·sta lobster • crayfish
arancini ⓜ pl a·ran·*chee*·nee rice balls stuffed with a meat mixture
aringa ⓕ a·*reen*·ga herring
arista ⓕ a·*ree*·sta cured, cooked pork meat
aromi ⓜ pl a·*ro*·mee aromatic herbs • spices

- b -

babà ⓜ ba·*ba* dessert containing sultanas
baccalà ⓜ ba·ka·*la* dried salted cod
baci ⓜ pl ba·chee 'kisses' – type of chocolate • type of pastry or biscuit
bagna ⓕ **cauda** ban·ya cow·da anchovy, olive oil & garlic dip served with raw vegetables
basilico ⓜ ba·*zee*·lee·ko basil
ben cotto/a ⓜ/ⓕ ben *ko*·to/a well done
besciamella ⓕ be·sha·*me*·la white sauce
bevande ⓕ pl be·*van*·de drinks
bibite ⓕ pl *bee*·bee·te soft drinks
birra ⓕ *bee*·ra beer
bistecca ⓕ bees·*te*·ka steak
bollito/a ⓜ/ⓕ bo·*lee*·to boiled
braciola ⓕ bra·*cho*·la chop
brioche ⓜ bree·*osh* breakfast pastry
brodo ⓜ *bro*·do broth

bruschetta ① broos·*ke*·ta toasted bread with olive oil & various toppings

budino ⓜ boo·*dee*·no milk-based pudding

busecca ① boo·*ze*·ka tripe

- c -

cacciucco ⓜ ka·*choo*·ko seafood stew with wine, garlic & herbs

calzone ⓜ kal·*tso*·ne fried or baked flat bread made with two thin sheets of pasta stuffed with any number of ingredients

cannella ① ka·*ne*·la cinnamon

cannelloni ⓜ pl ka·ne·*lo*·nee tubes of pasta stuffed with spinach, minced roast veal, ham, eggs, parmesan & spices

cantarelli ⓜ pl kan·ta·*re*·lee chanterelle mushrooms

cantucci ⓜ pl kan·*too*·chee crunchy, hard biscuits made with aniseed & almonds

caponata ① ka·po·*na*·ta eggplant with a tomato sauce

carciofi ⓜ pl kar·*cho*·fee artichokes

ciabatta ① cha·*ba*·ta crisp, flat & long bread

cioccolato ⓜ cho·ko·*la*·to chocolate

coda ① *ko*·da tail • angler fish

conchiglie ① pl kon·*kee*·lye pasta shells

condimento ⓜ kon·dee·*men*·to condiment • seasoning • dressing

contorni ⓜ pl kon·*tor*·nee side dishes • vegetables

costine ① pl kos·*tee*·ne ribs

cozze ① pl *ko*·tse mussels

crespella ① kres·*pe*·la a thin fritter

crostata ① kro·*sta*·ta fruit tart •

crust

crostini ⓜ pl kro·*stee*·nee slices of bread toasted with savoury toppings

crudo/a ⓜ/① *kroo*·do/a raw

- d -

della casa de·la *ka*·za 'of the house' – house speciality

digestivi ⓜ pl dee·jes·*tee*·vee digestifs

dolci ⓜ pl *dol*·chee desserts • sweets

- e -

erbe ① pl *er*·be herbs

- f -

fagiano ⓜ fa·*ja*·no pheasant

fagioli ⓜ pl fa·*jo*·lee beans

farcito/a ⓜ/① far·*chee*·to stuffed

farfalle ① pl far·*fa*·le butterfly-shaped pasta

farinata ① fa·ree·*na*·ta thin, flat bread made from chickpea flour

fetta ① *fe*·ta a slice

fettuccine ① pl fe·too·*chee*·ne long ribbon-shaped pasta

filetto ⓜ fee·*le*·to fillet

focaccia ① fo·*ka*·cha flat bread often filled or topped with cheese, ham, vegetables & other ingredients

formaggio ⓜ for·*ma*·jo cheese

fragole ① pl *fra*·go·le strawberries

fresco/a ⓜ/① *fres*·ko/a fresh

frittata ① free·*ta*·ta thick omelette slice, served hot or cold

frittelle ① pl free·*te*·le fritters

fritto/a ⓜ/ⓕ *free*·to/a fried
frumento ⓜ froo·*men*·to wheat
frutta ⓕ *froo*·ta fruit
frutti ⓜ pl **di mare** *froo*·tee dee *ma*·re seafood
funghi ⓜ pl *foon*·gee mushrooms

- g -

gambero ⓜ *gam*·be·ro prawn • shrimp
gamberoni ⓜ pl gam·be·*ro*·nee prawns
gelato ⓜ je·*la*·to ice cream
gnocchi ⓜ pl *nyo*·kee small dumplings – most commonly potato dumplings
gorgonzola ⓕ gor·gon·*dzo*·la spicy, sweet, creamy blue vein cow's milk cheese
granita ⓕ gra·*nee*·ta finely crushed flavoured ice
grappa ⓕ *gra*·pa distilled grape must

- i -

insalata ⓕ een·sa·*la*·ta salad
involtini ⓜ pl een·vol·*tee*·nee stuffed rolls of meat or fish

- l -

lenticchie ⓕ pl len·*tee*·kye lentils
lievito ⓜ *lye*·vee·to yeast
limone ⓜ lee·*mo*·ne lemon
lingua ⓕ *leen*·gwa tongue
linguine ⓕ pl leen·*gwee*·ne long thin ribbons of pasta
liquori ⓜ pl lee·*kwo*·ree spirits
luganega ⓕ loo·*ga*·ne·ga pork sausage
lumache ⓕ pl loo·*ma*·ke snails

- m -

maccheroni ⓜ pl ma·ke·*ro*·nee any tube pasta
marinato/a ⓜ/ⓕ ma·ree·*na*·to/a marinated
mascarpone ⓜ mas·kar·*po*·ne very soft & creamy cheese
melanzane ⓕ pl me·lan·*dza*·ne eggplants • aubergines
minestra ⓕ mee·*ne*·stra general word for soup
minestrone ⓜ mee·ne·*stro*·ne traditional vegetable soup
misto/a ⓜ/ⓕ *mees*·to/a mixed

- n -

noce ⓕ *no*·che nut • walnut
non troppo cotto/a ⓜ/ⓕ non *tro*·po *ko*·to/a medium rare

- o -

olio ⓜ *o*·lyo oil (almost always olive oil)
ossobuco ⓜ o·so·*boo*·ko veal shanks
ostriche ⓕ pl os·*tree*·ke oysters

- p -

pancetta ⓕ pan·*che*·ta salt-cured bacon
pane ⓜ *pa*·ne bread
panino ⓜ pa·*nee*·no bread roll
panzanella ⓕ pan·tsa·*ne*·la tomato, onion, garlic, olive oil, bread & basil salad
pasti leggeri ⓜ pl *pas*·tee le·*je*·ree light meals
patate ⓕ pl pa·*ta*·te potatoes

pecorino ⓜ **(romano)** pe·ko·ree·no (ro·ma·no) hard & spicy cheese made from ewe's milk

penne ⓕ pl pe·ne short & tubular pasta

peperoncini ⓜ pl pe·pe·ron·chee·nee hot chilli

peperoni ⓜ pl pe·pe·ro·nee peppers • capsicum

pesto ⓜ pes·to paste made from garlic, basil, pine nuts & parmesan

poco cotto/a ⓜ/ⓕ po·ko ko·to/a rare

polenta ⓕ po·len·ta corn meal porridge

polpette ⓜ pol·pe·te meatballs

pomodori ⓜ pl po·mo·do·ree tomatoes

primi piatti ⓜ pl pree·mee pya·tee entrees

prosciutto ⓜ pro·shoo·to basic term for many types of thinly sliced ham

– q –

quattro formaggi kwa·tro for·ma·jee pasta sauce with four different cheeses

quattro stagioni kwa·tro sta·jo·nee pizza with different toppings on each quarter

– r –

ragù ⓜ ra·goo generally a meat sauce but sometimes vegetarian

ravioli ⓜ pl ra·vee·o·lee pasta squares usually stuffed with meat, parmesan cheese & breadcrumbs

rigatoni ⓜ pl ree·ga·to·nee short, fat tubes of pasta

ripieno ⓜ ree·pye·no stuffing

riso ⓜ ree·zo rice

risotto ⓜ ree·zo·to rice dish slowly cooked in broth to a creamy consistency

rucola ⓕ roo·ko·la rocket

– s –

salsa ⓕ sal·sa sauce

salsiccia ⓕ sal·see·cha sausage

secondi piatti ⓜ pl se·kon·dee pya·tee main courses

spaghetti ⓜ pl spa·ge·tee ubiquitous long thin strands of pasta

spalla ⓕ spa·la shoulder

speck ⓜ spek type of smoked ham

suppa ⓕ soo·pa soup

– t –

tacchino ⓜ ta·kee·no turkey

tagliatelle ⓕ ta·lya·te·le long, ribbon-shaped pasta

tartufo ⓜ tar·too·fo truffle (mushroom)

tiramisù ⓜ tee·ra·mee·soo sponge cake soaked in coffee & arranged in layers with mascarpone, then sprinkled with cocoa

torta ⓕ tor·ta cake • tart • pie

tortellini ⓜ pl tor·te·lee·nee pasta filled with meat, parmesan & egg

– u –

uova ⓜ pl wo·va eggs

uva ⓕ pl oo·va grapes

– v –

verdure ⓕ pl ver·doo·re vegetables

vini ⓜ pl **bianchi** vee·nee byan·kee white wines

vini ⓜ pl **da dessert** *vee·nee da de·sert* dessert wines

vini ⓜ pl **della casa** *vee·nee de·la ka·sa* house wines

vini ⓜ pl **frizzanti** *vee·nee free·tsan·tee* sparkling wines

vini ⓜ pl **rosati** *vee·nee ro·sa·tee* rose wines

vini ⓜ pl **rossi** *vee·nee ro·see* red wines

vitello ⓜ *vee·te·lo* veal

vongole ⓕ pl *von·go·le* clams

~ Z ~

zucca ⓕ *tsoo·ka* pumpkin

zucchero ⓜ *tsoo·ke·ro* sugar

zuppa ⓕ *tsoo·pa* soup

Sightseeing

⩵ Fast Phrases

When's the museum open?	Quando è aperto il museo? *kwan*·do e a·*per*·to eel moo·*ze*·o
When's the next tour?	A che ora parte la prossima gita? a ke *o*·ra *par*·te la *pro*·see·ma *jee*·ta
Can I take photos?	Posso fare delle foto? *po*·so *fa*·re *de*·le *fo*·to

Planning

Do you have information on local sights?	Avete delle informazioni su posti locali? a·*ve*·te *de*·le een·for·ma·*tsyo*·nee soo *pos*·tee lo·*ka*·lee
I have only (one day).	Ho solo (un giorno). o *so*·lo (oon *jor*·no)
I'd like to see ...	Vorrei vedere ... vo·*ray* ve·*de*·re ...

| I'd like to hire a local guide. | Vorrei ingaggiare una guida del posto. vo·*ray* een·ga·*ja*·re *oo*·na *gwee*·da del *po*·sto |
| | |

| ✂ | Are there guides? | Avete guide? a·*ve*·te *gwee*·de |

Questions

What's that?	Cos'è? ko·*ze*
How old is it?	Quanti anni ha? *kwan*·tee *a*·nee a
Who made it?	Chi l'ha fatto? kee la *fa*·to
Can I take a photo (of you)?	Posso fare una foto (di Lei/tu)? pol/inf *po*·so *fa*·re *oo*·na *fo*·to (dee lay/too)
Could you take a photo of me?	Può farmi una foto? pwo *far*·mee *oo*·na *fo*·to

---

PHRASE BUILDER

I'd like a/an ...	Vorrei ...	vo·*ray* ...
audio set	un auricolare	oo·now·ree·ko·*la*·re
catalogue	un catalogo	oon ka·*ta*·lo·go
guidebook (in English)	una guida (in inglese)	*oo*·na *gwee*·da (ee·neen·*gle*·ze)
local map	una cartina della zona	*oo*·na kar·*tee*·na *de*·la *dzo*·na

Getting In

What time does it open?	A che ora apre?	a ke *o*·ra *a*·pre
What time does it close?	A che ora chiude?	a ke *o*·ra kyoo·de
What's the admission charge?	Quant'è il prezzo d'ingresso?	kwan·te eel *pre*·tso deen·*gre*·so

PHRASE BUILDER

Is there a discount for ...?	C'è uno sconto per ...?	che *oo*·no *skon*·to per ...
children	bambini	bam·*bee*·nee
families	famiglie	fa·*mee*·lye
groups	gruppi	*groo*·pee
older people	persone anziane	per·*so*·ne an·*tsya*·ne
students	studenti	stoo·*den*·tee

Galleries & Museums

When's the gallery open?	Quando è aperta la galleria? *kwan*·do e a·*per*·ta la ga·le·*ree*·a
When's the museum open?	Quando è aperto il museo? *kwan*·do e a·*per*·to eel moo·*ze*·o
What's in the collection?	Quali sono le opere qui esposte? *kwa*·lee *so*·no le *o*·pe·re kwee es·*pos*·te
It's a/an ... exhibition.	È una mostra di ... e *oo*·na *mos*·tra dee ...

Forming Sentences

You don't need to memorise complete sentences; instead, simply use key words to get your meaning across. For example, you might know that *quando* kwan·do means 'when' in Italian. So if you've arranged a tour but don't know what time, just ask *Gita quando?* jee·ta kwan·do. Don't worry that you're not getting the whole sentence right – people will understand if you stick to the key words.

I like the works of ...	Mi piacciono le opere di ...
	mee pya·cho·no le o·pe·re
	dee ...

PHRASE BUILDER

... art	l'arte ...	lar·te ...
baroque	barocca	ba·ro·ka
modernist	modernista	mo·der·nee·sta
Renaissance	rinascimentale	ree·na·shee·men·ta·le
Romanesque	romanica	ro·ma·nee·ka

Tours

When's the next tour?	A che ora parte la prossima gita?
	a ke o·ra par·te la pro·see·ma jee·ta
When's the next excursion?	A che ora parte la prossima escursione?
	a ke o·ra par·te la pro·see·ma es·koor·syo·ne

55

Tours

Can you recommend a tour?	Può consigliare una gita turistica? pwo kon·see·*lya*·re oo·na *jee*·ta too·*ree*·stee·ka
Can you recommend a boat trip?	Può consigliare una gita in barca? pwo kon·see·*lya*·re oo·na *jee*·ta een *bar*·ka
Can you recommend a day trip?	Può consigliare una escursione in giornata? pwo kon·see·*lya*·re oo·na es·koor·*syo*·ne een jor·*na*·ta

Is food included?	È incluso il vitto? e een·*kloo*·zo eel *vee*·to
Is transport included?	È incluso il trasporto? e een·*kloo*·zo eel tras·*por*·to
Do I need to take ... with me?	Devo portare ... con me? *de*·vo por·*ta*·re ... kon me
How long is the tour?	Quanto dura la gita? *kwan*·to *doo*·ra la *jee*·ta
What time should we be back?	A che ora dovremmo ritornare? a ke o·ra dov·*re*·mo ree·tor·*na*·re
I've lost my group.	Ho perso il mio gruppo. o *per*·so eel *mee*·o *groo*·po

Shopping

⇒ Fast Phrases

Can I look at it?	Posso dare un'occhiata? *po·so da·re oo·no·kya·ta*
How much is it?	Quanto costa? *kwan·to kos·ta*
That's too expensive.	È troppo caro. *e tro·po ka·ro*

Looking For ...

Where's (the market)?	Dov'è (il mercato)? *do·ve (eel mer·ka·to)*
Where can I buy (locally produced goods)?	Dove posso comprare (oggetti di produzione locale)? *do·ve po·so kom·pra·re (o·je·tee dee pro·doo·tsyo·ne lo·ka·le)*

In the Shop

I'd like to buy ...	Vorrei comprare ... *vo·ray kom·pra·re ...*

57

Shops

Where would you go for bargains?	Dove andrebbe per oggetti economici? *do·ve an·dre·be per o·je·tee e·ko·no·mee·chee*
Where would you go for souvenirs?	Dove andrebbe per ricordini locali? *do·ve an·dre·be per ree·kor·dee·nee lo·ka·lee*

I'm just looking.	Sto solo guardando. *sto so·lo gwar·dan·do*
Can I look at it?	Posso dare un'occhiata? *po·so da·re oo·no·kya·ta*
What is this made from?	Questo con che cosa è fatto? *kwe·sto kon ke ko·za e fa·to*
Do you have any others?	Ne avete altri? *ne a·ve·te al·tree*
It's faulty.	È difettoso. *e dee·fe·to·zo*
It's broken.	È rotto. *e ro·to*
Does it have a guarantee?	Ha la garanzia? *a la ga·ran·tsee·a*
Can I have it wrapped, please?	Può incartarlo, per favore? *pwo een·kar·tar·lo per fa·vo·re*
Can I have a bag, please?	Può darmi un sacchetto, per favore? *pwo dar·mee oon sa·ke·to per fa·vo·re*

I'd like my money back, please.	Vorrei un rimborso, per favore.
	vo·*ray* oon reem·*bor*·so per fa·*vo*·re
I'd like to return this, please.	Vorrei restituire questo, per favore.
	vo·*ray* res·tee·*twee*·re *kwe*·sto per fa·*vo*·re

Paying & Bargaining

How much is this?	Quanto costa questo?
	kwan·to *kos*·ta *kwes*·to
✄ How much?	Quanto?
	kwan·to
It's ... euros.	È ... euro.
	e ... *ow*·ro
Can you write down the price?	Può scrivere il prezzo?
	pwo *skree*·ve·re eel *pre*·tso
That's too expensive.	È troppo caro.
	e *tro*·po *ka*·ro
Can you lower the price?	Può farmi lo sconto?
	pwo *far*·mee lo *skon*·to
Do you have something cheaper?	Ha qualcosa di meno costoso?
	a kwal·*ko*·za dee *me*·no kos·*to*·zo
I'll give you ...	Le offro ...
	le *o*·fro ...
Do you accept credit cards?	Accettate la carta di credito?
	a·che·*ta*·te la *kar*·ta dee *kre*·dee·to

Fast Talk **False Friends**

Some Italian words look like English words but have a different meaning altogether. For example, *firma* feer·ma is 'signature', not 'firm' (which is *ditta* dee·ta); *camera* ka·me·ra is 'bedroom', not 'camera' (which is *macchina fotografica* ma·kee·na fo·to·gra·fee·ka); *tasto* ta·sto is 'touch', not 'taste' (which is *gusto* goo·sto); and *locale* lo·ka·le is 'bar/venue' (not 'local' or 'nearby', which is *vicino/a* m/f vee·chee·no/a).

I'd like my change, please.	Vorrei il mio resto, per favore. vo·ray eel mee·o res·to per fa·vo·re
Can I have a receipt, please?	Può darmi una ricevuta, per favore? pwo dar·mee oo·na ree·che·voo·ta per fa·vo·re
✂ Receipt, please.	La ricevuta, per favore. la ree·che·voo·ta per fa·vo·re

Clothes & Shoes

I'm looking for shoes.	Sto cercando delle scarpe. sto cher·kan·do de·le skar·pe
I'm looking for underwear.	Sto cercando della biancheria intima. sto cher·kan·do de·la byan·ke·ree·a een·tee·ma

My size is small.	Sono una taglia piccola. *so*·no *oo*·na *ta*·lya *pee*·ko·la
My size is medium.	Sono una taglia media. *so*·no *oo*·na *ta*·lya *me*·dya
My size is large.	Sono una taglia forte. *so*·no *oo*·na *ta*·lya *for*·te
Can I try it on?	Potrei provarmelo? po·*tray* pro·*var*·me·lo
It doesn't fit.	Non va bene. non va *be*·ne

Books & Reading

Is there an English-language bookshop?	C'è una libreria specializzata in lingua inglese? che *oo*·na lee·bre·*ree*·a spe·cha·lee·*dza*·ta een *leen*·gwa een·*gle*·ze
Is there an English-language section?	C'è una sezione di lingua inglese? che *oo*·na se·*tsyo*·ne dee *leen*·gwa een·*gle*·ze
Do you have a book by ...?	Avete un libro di ...? a·*ve*·te oon *lee*·bro dee ...
I'd like a dictionary.	Vorrei un vocabolario. vo·*ray* oon vo·ka·bo·*la*·ryo
I'd like a newspaper (in English).	Vorrei un giornale (in inglese). vo·*ray* oon jor·*na*·le (een een·*gle*·ze)

> **Fast Talk** **Common Speech Fillers**
> You may often hear Italians use the word
> *cioè* cho·*e* when they speak. This literally means 'that is
> to say' and is a common filler in spoken Italian. Some
> other 'filler' words you might hear are *bene/beh* be·ne/be
> (well), *ecco* e·ko (so), *mah* ma (God knows) and *diciamolo*
> dee·*cha*·mo·lo (let's say).

Music & DVDs

I'd like a CD/DVD.	Vorrei un CD/DVD. vo·*ray* oon chee·*dee*/ dee·voo·*dee*
I'd like some headphones.	Vorrei delle cuffia. vo·*ray* de·le koo·fya
I heard a band called ...	Ho sentito un gruppo chiamato ... o sen·*tee*·to oon *groo*·po kya·*ma*·to ...
What's his/her best recording?	Qual'è la sua migliore incisione? kwa·*le* la *soo*·a mee·*lyo*·re een·chee·*zyo*·ne
Can I listen to this?	Potrei ascoltare questo? po·*tray* as·kol·*ta*·re *kwe*·sto
Which region is this DVD for?	Questo DVD a quale DVD Region appartiene? *kwe*·sto dee·voo·*dee* a *kwa*·le dee·voo·*dee* re·jon a·par·*tye*·ne

Entertainment

⇒ Fast Phrases

What's on tonight?	Che c'è in programma stasera? ke che een pro·*gra*·ma sta·*se*·ra
Where are the clubs?	Dove sono dei clubs? *do*·ve so·no day kloobs
(When/Where) shall we meet?	(A che ora/Dove) ci vediamo? (a ke o·*ra*/*do*·ve) chee ve·*dya*·mo

Going Out

What's there to do in the evenings?	Che c'è in programma di sera? ke che een pro·*gra*·ma dee se·ra
✂ **What's on?**	Cosa si fa? *ko*·za see fa
What's on today?	Cosa si fa oggi? *ko*·za see fa o·jee
What's on tonight?	Cosa si fa stasera? *ko*·za see fa sta·*se*·ra

Local Knowledge Clubs

Can you recommend bars?	Può consigliare dei locali? pwo kon·see·*lya*·re day lo·*ka*·lee
Can you recommend clubs?	Può consigliare dei clubs? pwo kon·see·*lya*·re day kloobs
Can you recommend gay venues?	Può consigliare dei locali gay? pwo kon·see·*lya*·re day lo·*ka*·lee ge

What's on this weekend?	Cosa si fa questo finesettimana? *ko*·za see fa *kwe*·sto fee·ne·se·tee·*ma*·na
Is there a local entertainment guide?	C'è una guida agli spettacoli in questa città? che *oo*·na *gwee*·da *a*·lyee spe·*ta*·ko·lee een *kwe*·sta chee·*ta*

Fast Talk Conversation Dos & Don'ts

Italians are great communicators so you shouldn't have too much trouble striking up a conversation. Try topics such as architecture, films, food and soccer. Italians don't shy away from discussing political and social issues either and might be interested in knowing your opinion on all kinds of topics. Even *il campionato* eel kam·pyo·*na*·to (football/soccer) takes on the dimensions of a serious political issue. Talking about the Mafia, Mussolini or the Vatican, however, could see the conversation come to a premature halt.

PHRASE BUILDER

I feel like going to a/the ...	Ho voglia d'andare ...	o *vo*·lya dan·*da*·re ...
bar	a un locale	a oon lo·*ka*·le
coffee bar	a un caffè	a oon ka·*fe*
concert	a un concerto	a oon kon·*cher*·to
movies	al cinema	al *chee*·nee·ma
nightclub	in un locale notturno	een oon lo·*ka*·le no·*toor*·no
party	a una festa	a *oo*·na *fes*·ta
restaurant	in un ristorante	een oon rees·to·*ran*·te
theatre	al teatro	al te·*a*·tro

Meeting Up

When shall we meet?	A che ora ci vediamo? a ke *o*·ra chee ve·*dya*·mo
Let's meet at (eight) o'clock.	Incontriamoci alle (otto). een·kon·*trya*·mo·chee *a*·le (*o*·to)
Where will we meet?	Dove ci vediamo? *do*·ve chee ve·*dya*·mo
Let's meet at the entrance.	Incontriamoci all'entrata. een·kon·*trya*·mo·chee a·len·*tra*·ta
I'll pick you up.	Ti/Vi vengo a prendere. **sg/pl** tee/vee *ven*·go a *pren*·de·re
Sorry, I'm late.	Scusa, sono in ritardo. *skoo*·za *so*·no een ree·*tar*·do

65

Practicalities

⇒ Fast Phrases

Where's the nearest ATM?	Dov'è il Bancomat più vicino? do·ve eel *ban*·ko·mat pyoo vee·*chee*·no
Is there wireless internet access here?	Qui c'è il collegamento Wi-Fi? kwee chay eel ko·le·ga·*men*·to wai·fai
Where's the toilet?	Dove sono i gabinetti? *do*·ve *so*·no ee ga·bee·*ne*·tee

Banking

Where's the bank?	Dov'è la banca? do·*ve* la *ban*·ka
What time does the bank open?	A che ora apre la banca? a ke *o*·ra *a*·pre la *ban*·ka
Where's the nearest ATM?	Dov'è il Bancomat più vicino? do·*ve* eel *ban*·ko·mat pyoo vee·*chee*·no
Where's the nearest foreign exchange office?	Dov'è il cambio più vicino? do·*ve* eel *kam*·byo pyoo vee·*chee*·no

Where can I (change money)?	Dove posso (cambiare denaro)? *do·ve po·so (kam·bya·re de·na·ro)*
I'd like to (withdraw money).	Vorrei (fare un prelievo). *vo·ray (fa·re oon pre·lye·vo)*
What's the exchange rate?	Quant'è il cambio? *kwan·te eel kam·byo*
What's the commission?	Quant'è la commissione? *kwan·te la ko·mee·syo·ne*

Phone/Mobile Phone

Where's the nearest public phone?	Dov'è il telefono pubblico più vicino? *do·ve eel te·le·fo·no poo·blee·ko pyoo vee·chee·no*
I'd like to buy a phonecard.	Vorrei comprare una scheda telefonica. *vo·ray kom·pra·re oo·na ske·da te·le·fo·nee·ka*
I want to make a call to (Belgium).	Vorrei fare una chiamata in (Belgio). *vo·ray fa·re oo·na kya·ma·ta een (bel·jo)*
I want to make a reverse-charge/collect call.	Vorrei fare una chiamata a carico del destinatario. *vo·ray fa·re oo·na kya·ma·ta a ka·ree·ko del des·tee·na·ta·ryo*
How much does a (three)-minute call cost?	Quanto costa una telefonata di (tre) minuti? *kwan·to kos·ta oo·na te·le·fo·na·tadee (tre) mee·noo·tee*

The number is ...	Il numero è ... eel *noo*·me·ro e ...
It's engaged.	La linea è occupata. la *lee*·ne·a e o·koo·*pa*·ta
I've been cut off.	È caduta la linea. e ka·*doo*·ta la *lee*·ne·a
I'd like a charger for my phone.	Vorrei un caricabatterie. vo·*ray* oon ka·ree·ka·ba·te·*ree*·e
I'd like a SIM card for your network.	Vorrei un SIM card per la vostra rete telefonica. vo·*ray* oon seem kard per la *vos*·tra *re*·te te·le·*fo*·nee·ka

Internet

Where's the local internet cafe?	Dove si trova l'Internet point? *do*·ve see *tro*·va leen·ter·net poynt
Is there wireless internet access here?	Qui c'è il collegamento Wi-Fi? kwee chay eel ko·le·ga·*men*·to wai·fai
Can I connect my laptop here?	Posso collegare il mio portatile? *po*·so ko·le·*ga*·re eel *mee*·o por·ta·*tee*·le
Do you have headphones (with a microphone)?	Avete una cuffia (con microfono)? a·*ve*·te oo·na *koo*·fya (kon mee·*kro*·fo·no)
How do I log on?	Come posso accedere? *ko*·me *po*·so a·*che*·de·re

PHRASE BUILDER

I'd like to ...	Vorrei ...	vo·ray ...
burn a CD	masterizzare un CD	mas·te·ree·tsa·re oon chee·dee
check my email	controllare il mio email	kon·tro·la·re eel mee·e e·mayl
download my photos	scaricare le mie foto	ska·ree·ka·re le mee·e fo·to
use a printer	usare una stampante	oo·za·re oo·na stam·pan·te
use a scanner	scandire	skan·dee·re
use Skype	usare Skype	oo·za·re skaip

How much per hour?	Quanto costa all'ora?
	kwan·to *kos*·ta a·*lo*·ra

How much per page?	Quanto costa a pagina?
	kwan·to *kos*·ta a *pa*·jee·na

It's crashed.	Si è bloccato.
	see e blo·*ka*·to

I've finished.	Ho finito.
	o fee·*nee*·to

Can I connect (my camera) to this computer?	Posso collegare (la mia macchina fotografica) a questo computer?
	po·so ko·le·*ga*·re (la *mee*·a *ma*·kee·na fo·to·*gra*·fee·ka) a *kwe*·sto kom·*pyoo*·ter

Emergencies

Help!	Aiuto!
	a·*yoo*·to

Stop!	Fermi! *fer*·mee
Go away!	Vai via! vai *vee*·a
Leave me alone!	Lasciami in pace! *la*·sha·mee een *pa*·che
Thief!	Ladro! *la*·dro
Fire!	Al fuoco! al *fwo*·ko
Watch out!	Attenzione! a·ten·*tsyo*·ne
It's an emergency!	È un'emergenza! e oo·ne·mer·*jen*·tsa
Call the police!	Chiami la polizia! kya·mee la po·lee·*tsee*·a
Call a doctor!	Chiami un medico! kya·mee oon *me*·dee·ko

Fast Talk — Understanding Italian

Most sentences are composed of several words (or parts of words) serving various grammatical functions, as well as those that carry meaning (primarily nouns and verbs). If you're finding it hard to understand what someone is saying to you, listen out for the nouns and verbs to work out the context – this shouldn't be hard as they are usually more emphasised in speech. If you're still having trouble, a useful phrase to know is *Può/Puoi parlare più lentamente, per favore?* **pol/inf** pwo/pwoy par·*la*·re pyoo len·ta·*men*·te per fa·*vo*·re (Please speak more slowly).

There's been an accident.	C'è stato un incidente.
	che *sta*·to oon een·chee·*den*·te
Do you have a first-aid kit?	Avete una cassetta di pronto soccorso?
	a·*ve*·te *oo*·na ka·*se*·ta dee *pron*·to so·*kor*·so
Can you help me, please?	Mi può aiutare, per favore?
	mee pwo a·yoo·*ta*·re per fa·*vo*·re
✂ **Please help!**	Per favore aiutate!
	per fa·*vo*·re a·yoo·*ta*·te
I have to use the telephone.	Devo fare una telefonata.
	de·vo *fa*·re *oo*·na te·le·fo·*na*·ta
Where are the toilets?	Dove sono i gabinetti?
	do·ve *so*·no ee ga·bee·*ne*·tee
I'm lost.	Mi sono perso/a. **m/f**
	mee *so*·no *per*·so/a

Police

Where's the police station?	Dov'è il posto di polizia?
	do·*ve* eel *pos*·to dee po·lee·*tsee*·a
I've been raped.	Sono stato/a violentato/a. **m/f**
	so·no *sta*·to/a vyo·len·*ta*·to/a
I've been robbed.	Sono stato/a derubato/a. **m/f**
	so·no *sta*·to/a de·roo·*ba*·to/a
I've lost (my passport).	Ho perso (il mio passaporto).
	o *per*·so (eel *mee*·o pa·sa·*por*·to)
I've lost (my money).	Ho perso (il mio denaro).
	o *per*·so (eel *mee*·o de·*na*·ro)

(My bag) was stolen.	Mi hanno rubato (la mia borsa). mee *a*·no roo·*ba*·to (la *mee*·a *bor*·sa)
I want to contact my embassy.	Vorrei contattare la mia ambasciata. vo·*ray* kon·ta·*ta*·re la *mee*·a am·ba·*sha*·ta
I want to contact my consulate.	Vorrei contattare il mio consolato. vo·*ray* kon·ta·*ta*·re eel *mee*·o kon·so·*la*·to
I have insurance.	Ho l'assicurazione. o la·see·koo·ra·*tsyo*·ne

Health

Where's the nearest chemist?	Dov'è la farmacia più vicina? do·*ve* la far·ma·*chee*·a pyoo vee·*chee*·na
Where's the nearest dentist?	Dov'è il/la dentista più vicino/a? m/f do·*ve* eel/la den·*tee*·sta pyoo vee·*chee*·no/a
Where's the nearest hospital?	Dov'è l'ospedale più vicino? do·*ve* los·pe·*da*·le pyoo vee·*chee*·no
I need a doctor (who speaks English).	Ho bisogno di un medico (che parli inglese). o bee·*zo*·nyo dee oon *me*·dee·ko (ke *par*·lee een·*gle*·ze)

Could I see a female doctor?	Posso vedere una dottoressa? *po·so ve·de·re oo·na do·to·re·sa*
I'm sick.	Mi sento male. *mee sen·to ma·le*
It hurts here.	Mi fa male qui. *mee fa ma·le kwee*
I've been vomiting.	Ho vomitato alcune volte. *o vo·mee·ta·to al·koo·ne vol·te*
I feel dizzy.	Ho il capogiro. *o eel ka·po·gee·ro*
I feel nauseous.	Ho la nausea. *o la now·ze·a*

PHRASE BUILDER

I have (a/an) ...	Ho ...	o ...
cold	un raffreddore	oon ra·fre·do·re
cough	la tosse	la to·se
diarrhoea	la diarrea	la dee·a·re·a
fever	la febbre	la fe·bre
headache	mal di testa	mal dee tes·ta
infection	un'infezione	oon een·fe·tsyo·ne
rash	uno sfogo	oo·no sfo·go
toothache	mal di denti	mal dee den·tee

| I'm on medication for ... | Prendo la medicina per ...
 pren·do la me·dee·chee·na per ... |
| I need something for ... | Ho bisogno di qualcosa per ...
 o bee·zo·nyo dee kwal·ko·za per ... |

73

Fast Talk Body Language

Italians are emotionally demonstrative so expect to see lots of cheek-kissing among acquaintances, embraces between good friends and lingering handshakes. Both men and women may walk along arm-in-arm. Pushing and shoving in busy places is not considered rude, so don't be offended by it. Don't ever point at anyone with your little finger and index finger, as it's considered a great insult. Also be aware that respectful behaviour is expected in churches. Women should avoid exposing too much flesh – wearing shorts or skimpy tops is considered disrespectful.

My prescription is ...	Mi ricetta è ... mee ree·*che*·ta e ...
I'm allergic (to antibiotics).	Sono allergico/a (agli antibiotici). m/f *so*·no a·*ler*·jee·ko/a (*a*·lyee an·tee·bee·o·tee·chee)
I have a skin allergy.	Ho un'allergia alla pelle. o oo·na·ler·*jee*·a a·la *pe*·le

Dictionary

ENGLISH *to* ITALIAN

inglese – italiano

Nouns in this dictionary, and adjectives affected by gender, have their gender indicated by ⓜ or ⓕ. If it's a plural noun, you'll also see pl. Where a word that could be either a noun or a verb has no gender indicated, it's a verb.

- a -

accident incidente ⓜ een·chee·*den*·te
accommodation alloggio ⓜ a·*lo*·jo
afternoon pomeriggio ⓜ
po·me·*ree*·jo
air-conditioned ad aria condizionata
ad *a*·rya kon·dee·*tsyo*·na·ta
airport aeroporto ⓜ a·e·ro·*por*·to
airport tax tassa ⓕ aeroportuale
ta·sa a·e·ro·por·*twa*·le
alarm clock sveglia ⓕ *sve*·lya
alcohol alcol ⓜ *al*·kol
antique pezzo ⓜ di antiquariato
pe·tso dee an·tee·kwa·*rya*·to
appointment appuntamento ⓜ
a·poon·ta·*men*·to
arrivals arrivi ⓜ pl a·*ree*·vee

art gallery galleria ⓕ d'arte
ga·le·*ree*·a *dar*·te
ashtray portacenere ⓜ
por·ta·*che*·ne·re
at a a
ATM Bancomat ⓜ *ban*·ko·mat

- b -

B&W (film) in bianco e nero een
byan·ko e *ne*·ro
baby bimbo/a ⓜ/ⓕ *beem*·bo/a
back (body) schiena ⓕ *skye*·na
backpack zaino ⓜ *dzai*·no
bad cattivo/a ⓜ/ⓕ ka·*tee*·vo/a
bag (general) borsa ⓕ *bor*·sa
bag (shopping) sacchetto ⓜ sa·*ke*·to
baggage bagaglio ⓜ ba·*ga*·lyo

baggage allowance bagaglio ⓜ consentito ba·ga·lyo kon·sen·tee·to

baggage claim ritiro ⓜ bagagli ree·tee·ro ba·ga·lyee

bakery panetteria ⓕ pa·ne·te·ree·a

Band-Aids cerotti ⓜ pl che·ro·tee

bank (money) banca ⓕ ban·ka

bank account conto ⓜ in banca kon·to een ban·ka

bath bagno ⓜ ba·nyo

bathroom bagno ⓜ ba·nyo

battery pila ⓕ pee·la

beach spiaggia ⓕ spya·ja

beautiful bello/a ⓜ/ⓕ be·lo/a

beauty salon parrucchiere ⓜ pa·roo·kye·re

bed letto ⓜ le·to

bedroom camera ⓕ da letto ka·me·ra da le·to

beer birra ⓕ bee·ra

bicycle bicicletta ⓕ bee·chee·kle·ta

big grande gran·de

bill (account) conto ⓜ kon·to

birthday compleanno ⓜ kom·ple·a·no

black nero/a ⓜ/ⓕ ne·ro/a

blanket coperta ⓕ ko·per·ta

blood group gruppo ⓜ sanguigno groo·po san·gwee·nyo

blue (dark) blu bloo

blue (light) azzurro/a ⓜ/ⓕ a·dzoo·ro/a

boarding house pensione ⓕ pen·syo·ne

boarding pass carta ⓕ d'imbarco kar·ta deem·bar·ko

boat barca ⓕ bar·ka

book libro ⓜ lee·bro

book (make a booking) prenotare pre·no·ta·re

booked out completo/a ⓜ/ⓕ kom·ple·to/a

bookshop libreria ⓕ lee·bre·ree·a

border confine ⓜ kon·fee·ne

bottle bottiglia ⓕ bo·tee·lya

box scatola ⓕ ska·to·la

boy bambino ⓜ bam·bee·no

boyfriend ragazzo ⓜ ra·ga·tso

bra reggiseno ⓕ re·jee·se·no

bread pane ⓜ pa·ne

briefcase valigetta ⓕ va·lee·je·ta

broken rotto/a ⓜ/ⓕ ro·to/a

brother fratello ⓜ fra·te·lo

brown marrone ⓜ/ⓕ ma·ro·ne

building edificio ⓜ e·dee·fee·cho

bus (city) autobus ⓜ ow·to·boos

bus (coach) pullman ⓜ pool·man

bus station stazione ⓕ d'autobus sta·tsyo·ne dow·to·boos

bus stop fermata ⓕ d'autobus fer·ma·ta dow·to·boos

business affari ⓜ pl a·fa·ree

business class classe ⓕ business kla·se beez·nes

butcher's shop macelleria ⓕ ma·che·le·ree·a

~ C ~

cafe bar ⓜ bar

camera macchina ⓕ fotografica ma·kee·na fo·to·gra·fee·ka

can (tin) scatola ⓕ ska·to·la

cancel cancellare kan·che·la·re

car macchina ⓕ ma·kee·na

car hire autonoleggio ⓜ ow·to·no·le·jo

car owner's title libretto ⓜ di circolazione lee·bre·to dee cheer·ko·la·tsyo·ne

car registration bollo ⓜ di circolazione bo·lo dee cheer·ko·la·tsyo·ne

cash soldi ⓜ pl sol·dee

cashier cassiere/a ⓜ/ⓕ ka·sye·re/a

chairlift (skiing) seggiovia ⓕ se·jo·vee·a

change cambiare kam·bya·re

change (coins) spiccioli ⓜ pl spee·cho·lee

change (money) resto ⓜ res·to

check controllare kon·tro·*la*·re

check (bank) assegno ⓜ a·*se*·nyo

check (bill) conto ⓜ *kon*·to

check-in (airport) accetazione ⓕ a·che·ta·*tsyo*·ne

check-in (hotel) registrazione ⓕ re·jee·stra·*tsyo*·ne

cheque assegno ⓜ a·*se*·nyo

child bambino/a ⓜ/ⓕ bam·*bee*·no/a

church chiesa ⓕ *kye*·za

cigarette lighter accendino ⓜ a·chen·*dee*·no

city città ⓕ chee·*ta*

clean pulito/a ⓜ/ⓕ poo·*lee*·to/a

cleaning pulizia ⓕ poo·lee·*tsee*·a

cloakroom guardaroba ⓜ gwar·da·*ro*·ba

closed chiuso/a ⓜ/ⓕ *kyoo*·zo/a

clothing abbigliamento ⓜ a·bee·lya·*men*·to

coat cappotto ⓜ ka·*po*·to

coffee caffè ⓜ ka·*fe*

coins monete ⓕ pl mo·*ne*·te

cold freddo/a ⓜ/ⓕ *fre*·do/a

comfortable comodo/a ⓜ/ⓕ *ko*·mo·do/a

company (firm) ditta ⓕ *dee*·ta

condom preservativo ⓜ pre·zer·va·*tee*·vo

confirm (a booking) confermare kon·fer·*ma*·re

connection (transport) coincidenza ⓕ ko·een·chee·*den*·tsa

convenience store alimentari ⓜ a·lee·men·*ta*·ree

cook cucinare koo·chee·*na*·re

cough tossire to·*see*·re

countryside campagna ⓕ kam·*pa*·nya

cover charge (restaurant) coperto ⓜ ko·*per*·to

cover charge (venue) ingresso ⓜ een·*gre*·so

craft (product) pezzo ⓜ d'artigianato *pe*·tso dar·tee·ja·*na*·to

credit card carta ⓕ di credito *kar*·ta dee *kre*·dee·to

currency exchange cambio ⓜ valuta *kam*·byo va·*loo*·ta

customs dogana ⓕ do·*ga*·na

-d-

date (day) data ⓕ *da*·ta

date of birth data ⓕ di nascita *da*·ta dee *na*·shee·ta

daughter figlia ⓕ *fee*·lya

day giorno ⓜ *jor*·no

day after tomorrow dopodomani do·po·do·*ma*·nee

day before yesterday altro ieri ⓜ *al*·tro *ye*·ree

delay ritardo ⓜ ree·*tar*·do

delicatessen salumeria ⓕ sa·loo·me·*ree*·a

depart partire par·*tee*·re

department store magazzino ⓜ *gran*·de ma·ga·*dzee*·no

departure partenza ⓕ par·*ten*·tsa

diaper pannolino ⓜ pa·no·*lee*·no

dictionary vocabolario ⓜ vo·ka·bo·*la*·ryo

dining car carrozza ⓕ ristorante ka·*ro*·tsa rees·to·*ran*·te

dinner cena ⓕ *che*·na

direct diretto/a ⓜ/ⓕ dee·*re*·to/a

dirty sporco/a ⓜ/ⓕ *spor*·ko/a

discount sconto ⓜ *skon*·to

doctor medico ⓜ *me*·dee·ko

dog cane ⓜ *ka*·ne

double bed letto ⓜ matrimoniale *le*·to ma·tree·mo·*nya*·le

double room camera ⓕ doppia *ka*·mer·a *do*·pya

dress abito ⓜ *a*·bee·to

drink bere *be*·re

drivers licence patente ⓕ (di guida) pa·*ten*·te (dee *gwee*·da)

drunk ubriaco/a ⓜ/ⓕ oo·bree·*a*·ko/a

dry secco/a ⓜ/ⓕ *se*·ko/a

-e-

each ciascuno/a ⓜ/ⓕ chas·*koo*·no/a
early presto ⓜ/ⓕ *pres*·to
east est ⓜ est
economy class classe ⓕ turistica
kla·se too·ree·*stee*·ka
embassy ambasciata ⓕ
am·ba·*sha*·ta
English inglese een·*gle*·ze
enough abbastanza a·bas·*tan*·tsa
entry entrata ⓕ en·*tra*·ta
evening sera ⓕ *se*·ra
everything tutto ⓜ *too*·to
exchange cambiare kam·*bya*·re
exhibition esposizione ⓕ
es·po·zee·*tsyo*·ne
exit uscita ⓕ oo·*shee*·ta
expensive caro/a ⓜ/ⓕ *ka*·ro/a
express mail posta ⓕ prioritaria
pos·ta pree·o·ree·*ta*·rya

-f-

fall (autumn) autunno ⓜ ow·*too*·no
family famiglia ⓕ fa·*mee*·lya
fashion moda ⓕ *mo*·da
fast veloce ve·*lo*·che
father padre ⓜ *pa*·dre
ferry traghetto ⓜ tra·*ge*·to
fever febbre ⓕ *fe*·bre
film (cinema) film ⓜ feelm
fine (payment) multa ⓕ *mool*·ta
finger dito ⓜ *dee*·to
first class prima classe ⓕ *pree*·ma
kla·se
fish shop pescheria ⓕ pe·ske·*ree*·a
flight volo ⓜ *vo*·lo
floor (storey) piano ⓜ *pya*·no
flu influenza ⓕ een·floo·*en*·tsa
footpath marciapiede ⓜ
mar·cha·*pye*·de
foreign straniero/a ⓜ/ⓕ
stra·*nye*·ro/a
forest foresta ⓕ fo·*res*·ta

free (gratis) gratuito/a ⓜ/ⓕ
gra·too·ee·to/a
fresh fresco/a ⓜ/ⓕ *fres*·ko/a
friend amico/a ⓜ/ⓕ a·*mee*·ko/a

-g-

garden giardino ⓜ jar·*dee*·no
gas (for cooking) gas ⓜ gaz
gas (petrol) benzina ⓕ ben·*dzee*·na
gift regalo ⓜ re·*ga*·lo
girl ragazza ⓕ ra·*ga*·tsa
girlfriend ragazza ⓕ ra·*ga*·tsa
glasses (spectacles) occhiali ⓜ pl
o·*kya*·lee
gloves guanti ⓜ pl *gwan*·tee
go andare an·*da*·re
gold oro ⓜ *o*·ro
green verde *ver*·de
grey grigio/a ⓜ/ⓕ *gree*·jo/a
grocery drogheria ⓕ dro·ge·*ree*·a
guesthouse pensione ⓕ pen·*syo*·ne
guided tour visita ⓕ guidata
vee·zee·ta gwee·*da*·ta

-h-

handsome bello/a ⓜ/ⓕ *be*·lo/a
heat caldo ⓜ *kal*·do
help aiutare a·yoo·*ta*·re
here qui kwee
hire noleggiare no·le·*ja*·re
holidays vacanze ⓕ pl va·*kan*·tse
honeymoon luna ⓕ di miele *loo*·na
dee *mye*·le
hospital ospedale ⓜ os·pe·*da*·le
hot caldo/a ⓜ/ⓕ *kal*·do/a
hotel albergo ⓜ al·*ber*·go
hour ora ⓕ *o*·ra
husband marito ⓜ ma·*ree*·to

-i-

identification documento ⓜ
d'identità do·koo·*men*·to dee·den·tee·*ta*

identification card (ID) carta ① d'identità *kar*·ta dee·den·tee·*ta*
ill malato/a ⓜ/① ma·*la*·to/a
included compreso/a ⓜ/① kom·*pre*·zo/a
information informazioni ① pl een·for·ma·*tsyo*·nee
insurance assicurazione ① a·see·koo·ra·*tsyo*·ne
intermission intervallo ⓜ een·ter·va·lo
internet cafe Internet point ⓜ een·ter·net poynt
interpreter interprete ⓜ/① een·*ter*·pre·te
itinerary itinerario ⓜ ee·tee·ne·*ra*·ryo

- *j* -

jacket giacca ① *ja*·ka
jeans jeans ⓜ pl jeens
jewellery gioielli ⓜ pl jo·*ye*·lee
jumper maglione ⓜ ma·*lyo*·ne

- *k* -

kind gentile jen·*tee*·le
kitchen cucina ① koo·*chee*·na

- *l* -

last ultimo/a ⓜ/① *ool*·tee·mo/a
late in ritardo een ree·*tar*·do
laundrette lavanderia ① a gettone la·van·de·*ree*·a je·*to*·ne
laundry lavanderia ① la·van·de·*ree*·a
leather cuoio ⓜ *kwo*·yo
left luggage (office) deposito ⓜ bagagli de·*po*·zee·to ba·*ga*·lyee
letter lettera ① *le*·te·ra
lift (elevator) ascensore ⓜ a·shen·*so*·re
locked chiuso/a ⓜ/① (a chiave) *kyoo*·zo/a (a *kya*·ve)
lost perso/a ⓜ/① *per*·so/a

luggage bagaglio ⓜ ba·*ga*·lyo
luggage lockers armadietti ⓜ pl per i bagagli ar·ma·*dye*·tee per ee ba·*ga*·lyee
lunch pranzo ⓜ *pran*·dzo

- *m* -

mail posta ① *pos*·ta
make-up trucco ⓜ *troo*·ko
man uomo ⓜ *wo*·mo
manager manager ⓜ *me*·nee·je
map pianta ① *pyan*·ta
market mercato ⓜ mer·*ka*·to
meat carne ① *kar*·ne
medicine medicina ① me·dee·*chee*·na
metro station stazione ① della metropolitana sta·*tsyo*·ne *de*·la me·tro·po·lee·*ta*·na
midnight mezzanotte ① me·dza·*no*·te
milk latte ⓜ *la*·te
mineral water acqua ① minerale *a*·kwa mee·ne·*ra*·le
mobile phone (telephone) cellulare ⓜ (te·*le*·fo·no) che·loo·*la*·re
modem modem ⓜ *mo*·dem
money denaro ⓜ de·*na*·ro
month mese ⓜ *me*·ze
morning mattina ① ma·*tee*·na
mother madre ① *ma*·dre
motorway (tollway) autostrada ① ow·to·*stra*·da
mountain montagna ① mon·*ta*·nya
museum museo ⓜ moo·*ze*·o
music musica ① *moo*·zee·ka

- *n* -

name nome ⓜ *no*·me
napkin tovagliolo ⓜ to·va·*lyo*·lo
nappy (diaper) pannolino ⓜ pa·no·*lee*·no
newsagency edicola ① e·*dee*·ko·la
newspaper giornale ⓜ jor·*na*·le

next prossimo/a ⓜ/ⓕ *pro·see·mo/a*
night notte ⓕ *no·te*
nonsmoking non fumatore *non foo·ma·to·re*
north nord ⓜ *nord*
now adesso *a·de·so*
number numero ⓜ *noo·me·ro*

~ o ~

oil olio ⓜ *o·lyo*
one-way (ticket) (un biglietto di) solo andata (oon bee·*lye*·to dee) *so·lo an·da·ta*
open aperto/a ⓜ/ⓕ *a·per·to/a*
opening hours orario ⓜ di apertura *o·ra·ryo dee a·per·too·ra*
orange (colour) arancione *a·ran·cho·ne*

~ p ~

painter pittore/pittrice ⓜ/ⓕ *pee·to·re/pee·tree·che*
painting (the art) pittura ⓕ *pee·too·ra*
pants pantaloni ⓜ pl *pan·ta·lo·nee*
pantyhose collant ⓜ pl *ko·lant*
paper carta ⓕ *kar·ta*
party (celebration) festa ⓕ *fes·ta*
passenger passeggero/a ⓜ/ⓕ *pa·se·je·ro/a*
passport passaporto ⓜ *pa·sa·por·to*
path sentiero ⓜ *sen·tye·ro*
penknife temperino ⓜ *tem·pe·ree·no*
pensioner pensionato/a ⓜ/ⓕ *pen·syo·na·to/a*
petrol benzina ⓕ *ben·dzee·na*
petrol station distributore ⓜ *dee·stree·boo·to·re*
phone book elenco ⓜ telefonico *e·len·ko te·le·fo·nee·ko*
phone box cabina ⓕ telefonica *ka·bee·na te·le·fo·nee·ka*
phrasebook vocabolarietto ⓜ *vo·ka·bo·la·rye·to*

picnic picnic ⓜ *peek·neek*
pillow cuscino ⓜ *koo·shee·no*
pillowcase federa ⓕ *fe·de·ra*
pink rosa ⓜ/ⓕ *ro·za*
platform binario ⓜ *bee·na·ryo*
play (theatre) commedia ⓕ *ko·me·dya*
police (civilian) polizia ⓕ *po·lee·tsee·a*
police (military) carabinieri ⓜ pl *ka·ra·bee·nye·ree*
police station posto ⓜ di polizia *pos·to dee po·lee·tsee·a*
post code codice ⓜ postale *ko·dee·che pos·ta·le*
post office ufficio ⓜ postale *oo·fee·cho pos·ta·le*
postcard cartolina ⓕ *kar·to·lee·na*
pound (money) sterlina ⓕ *ster·lee·na*
prescription ricetta ⓕ *ree·che·ta*
present (gift) regalo ⓜ *re·ga·lo*
price prezzo ⓜ *pre·tso*

~ q ~

quiet tranquillo/a ⓜ/ⓕ *tran·kwee·lo/a*

~ r ~

receipt ricevuta ⓕ *ree·che·voo·ta*
red rosso/a ⓜ/ⓕ *ro·so/a*
refund rimborso ⓜ *reem·bor·so*
repair riparare *ree·pa·ra·re*
return (ticket) (biglietto) di andata e ritorno (bee·*lye*·to) dee an·da·ta e ree·tor·no
right (direction) a destra *a de·stra*
room camera ⓕ *ka·me·ra*

~ s ~

safe cassaforte ⓕ *ka·sa·for·te*
sea mare ⓜ *ma·re*
season stagione ⓕ *sta·jo·ne*

seat (place) posto ⓜ *pos*·to
seatbelt cintura ⓕ di sicurezza
cheen·*too*·ra dee see·koo·*re*·tsa
self-service self-service self·*ser*·vees
service servizio ⓜ ser·*vee*·tsyo
service charge servizio ⓜ
ser·*vee*·tsyo
share (with) condividere
kon·dee·*vee*·de·re
shirt camicia ⓕ ka·*mee*·cha
shoes scarpe ⓕ pl *skar*·pe
shop negozio ⓜ ne·*go*·tsyo
shopping centre centro ⓜ
commerciale *chen*·tro ko·mer·*cha*·le
short (height) basso/a ⓜ/ⓕ *ba*·so/a
short (length) corto/a ⓜ/ⓕ *kor*·to/a
show mostrare mos·*tra*·re
shower doccia ⓕ *do*·cha
sick malato/a ⓜ/ⓕ ma·*la*·to/a
silk seta ⓕ *se*·ta
silver argento ⓜ ar·*jen*·to
single (man) celibe ⓜ *che*·lee·be
single (woman) nubile ⓕ *noo*·bee·le
single room camera ⓕ singola
ka·me·ra *seen*·go·la
sister sorella ⓕ so·*re*·la
size (general) dimensioni ⓕ pl
dee·men·*syo*·nee
skirt gonna ⓕ *go*·na
sleeping bag sacco ⓜ a pelo *sa*·ko
a *pe*·lo
sleeping car vagone ⓜ letto va·*go*·ne
le·to
slide (film) diapositiva ⓜ
dee·a·po·zee·*tee*·va
smoke fumare foo·*ma*·re
snack spuntino ⓜ spoon·*tee*·no
snow neve ⓕ *ne*·ve
socks calzini ⓜ pl cal·*tsee*·nee
son figlio ⓜ *fee*·lyo
soon fra poco fra *po*·ko
south sud ⓜ sood
spring (season) primavera ⓕ
pree·ma·*ve*·ra
square (town) piazza ⓕ *pya*·tsa

stairway scale ⓕ pl *ska*·le
stamp francobollo ⓜ fran·ko·*bo*·lo
stationer cartolaio ⓜ kar·to·*la*·yo
stolen rubato/a ⓜ/ⓕ roo·*ba*·to/a
student studente/studentessa ⓜ/ⓕ
stoo·*den*·te/stoo·den·*te*·sa
suitcase valigia ⓕ va·*lee*·ja
summer estate ⓕ es·*ta*·te
supermarket supermercato ⓜ
soo·per·mer·*ka*·to
surface mail posta ⓕ ordinaria
pos·ta or·dee·*na*·rya
sweater maglione ⓜ ma·*lyo*·ne
swim nuotare nwo·*ta*·re
swimming pool piscina ⓕ pee·*shee*·na

– t –

taxi stand posteggio ⓜ di tassi
po·*ste*·jo dee ta·*see*
ticket biglietto ⓜ bee·*lye*·to
ticket machine distributore ⓜ
automatico di biglietti
dee·stree·boo·*to*·re ow·to·*ma*·tee·ko
dee bee·*lye*·tee
ticket office biglietteria ⓕ
bee·lye·te·*ree*·a
timetable orario ⓜ o·*ra*·ryo
tip (gratuity) mancia ⓕ *man*·cha
today oggi o·jee
together insieme een·*sye*·me
tomorrow domani do·*ma*·nee
tour gita ⓕ *jee*·ta
tourist office ufficio ⓜ del turismo
oo·*fee*·cho del too·*reez*·mo
towel asciugamano ⓜ
a·shoo·ga·*ma*·no
train station stazione ⓕ (ferroviaria)
sta·*tsyo*·ne (fe·ro·*vyar*·ya)
transit lounge sala ⓕ di transito
sa·la dee *tran*·zee·to
travel agency agenzia ⓕ di viaggio
a·jen·*tsee*·a dee vee·*a*·jo
travellers cheque assegno ⓜ di
viaggio a·*se*·nyo dee vee·*a*·jo

trousers pantaloni ⓜ pl pan·ta·*lo*·nee
twin beds due letti *doo*·e *le*·tee

- u -

underwear biancheria ⓕ intima
byan·ke·*ree*·a *een*·tee·ma
urgent urgente ⓜ/ⓕ oor·*jen*·te

- v -

vacant libero/a ⓜ/ⓕ *lee*·be·ro/a
vacation vacanza ⓕ va·*kan*·tsa
validate convalidare kon·va·lee·*da*·re
vegetable verdura ⓕ ver·*doo*·ra
view vista ⓕ *vee*·sta

- w -

waiting room sala ⓕ d'attesa *sa*·la
da·te·sa
walk camminare ka·mee·*na*·re
warm tiepido/a ⓜ/ⓕ *tye*·pee·do/a
wash (something) lavare la·*va*·re
washing machine lavatrice ⓕ
la·va·*tree*·che

watch guardare gwar·*da*·re
water acqua ⓕ *a*·kwa
week settimana ⓕ se·tee·*ma*·na
west ovest ⓜ o·vest
when quando *kwan*·do
where dove *do*·ve
white bianco/a ⓜ/ⓕ *byan*·ko/a
who chi kee
why perché per·*ke*
wife moglie ⓕ *mo*·lye
window (car, plane) finestrino ⓜ
fee·nes·*tree*·no
window (general) finestra ⓕ
fee·*nes*·tra
wine vino ⓜ *vee*·no
winter inverno ⓜ een·*ver*·no
without senza *sen*·tsa
woman donna ⓕ *do*·na
wool lana ⓕ *la*·na

- y -

year anno ⓜ *a*·no
yesterday ieri ye·ree
youth hostel ostello ⓜ della gioventù
os·*te*·lo *de*·la jo·ven·*too*

Dictionary

ITALIAN *to* ENGLISH

italiano – inglese

Nouns in this dictionary, and adjectives affected by gender, have their gender indicated by ⓜ or ⓕ. If it's a plural noun, you'll also see pl. Where a word that could be either a noun or a verb has no gender indicated, it's a verb.

- a -

abbastanza a·bas·*tan*·tsa enough
abbigliamento ⓜ a·bee·lya·men·to clothing
abito ⓜ a·bee·to dress
accetazione ⓕ a·che·ta·tsyo·ne check-in (airport)
acqua ⓕ a·kwa water
acqua ⓕ **minerale** a·kwa mee·ne·ra·le mineral water
adesso a·de·so now
aeroporto ⓜ a·e·ro·por·to airport
affari ⓜ pl a·fa·ree business
agenzia ⓕ **di viaggio** a·jen·tsee·a dee vee·a·jo travel agency
aiutare a·yoo·ta·re help
albergo ⓜ al·ber·go hotel

alloggio ⓜ a·lo·jo accommodation
altro ieri ⓜ al·tro ye·ree day before yesterday
ambasciata ⓕ am·ba·sha·ta embassy
amico/a ⓜ/ⓕ a·mee·ko/a friend
anno ⓜ a·no year
aperto/a ⓜ/ⓕ a·per·to/a open
appuntamento ⓜ a·poon·ta·men·to appointment • date
arancia ⓕ a·ran·cha orange (fruit)
arancione a·ran·cho·ne orange (colour)
aria ⓕ **condizionata** a·rya kon·dee·tsyo·na·ta air-conditioning
armadietti ⓜ pl **per i bagagli** ar·ma·dye·tee per ee ba·ga·lyee luggage lockers
arrivi ⓜ pl a·ree·vee arrivals

83

assegno ⓜ **di viaggio** a·se·nyo dee vee·*a*·jo travellers cheque

assicurazione ① a·see·koo·ra·*tsyo*·ne insurance

autobus ⓜ *ow*·to·boos bus (city)

autonoleggio ⓜ ow·to·no·*le*·jo car hire

azzurro/a ⓜ/① a·*dzoo*·ro/a blue (light)

~ *b* ~

bagaglio ⓜ **consentito** ba·*ga*·lyo kon·sen·*tee*·to bagage allowance

bagaglio ⓜ **in eccedenza** ba·ga·lyo een e·che·*den*·tsa excess bagage

bagno ⓜ *ba*·nyo bath • bathroom

bambino/a ⓜ/① bam·*bee*·no/a child

Bancomat ⓜ *ban*·ko·mat automatic teller machine (ATM)

barca ① *bar*·ka boat

bebé ⓜ&① be·*be* baby

bello/a ⓜ/① *be*·lo/a beautiful • handsome • good (weather)

bere *be*·re drink

bevanda ① be·*van*·da drink (beverage)

biancheria ① **intima** byan·ke·*ree*·a een·tee·ma underwear

bianco/a ⓜ/① *byan*·ko/a white

bicicletta ① bee·chee·*kle*·ta bicycle

biglietteria ① bee·lye·te·*ree*·a ticket office

biglietto ⓜ **di andata e ritorno** bee·*lye*·to dee an·*da*·ta e ree·*tor*·no return ticket

bimbo/a ⓜ/① *beem*·bo/a baby

binario ⓜ bee·*na*·ryo platform

birra ① *bee*·ra beer

blu bloo blue (dark)

bollo ⓜ **di circolazione** *bo*·lo dee cheer·ko·la·*tsyo*·ne car registration

borsa ① *bor*·sa bag (general)

bottiglia ① bo·*tee*·lya bottle

~ *c* ~

cabina ① **telefonica** ka·*bee*·na te·le·*fo*·nee·ka phone box

caffè ⓜ ka·*fe* coffee

caldo/a ⓜ/① *kal*·do/a hot

calzini ⓜ pl kal·*tsee*·nee socks

cambiare kam·*bya*·re change

cambio ⓜ **valuta** ① *kam*·byo va·*loo*·ta currency exchange

camera ① **da letto** *ka*·me·ra da *le*·to bedroom

camera ① **doppia** *ka*·me·ra *do*·pya double room

camera ① **singola** *ka*·me·ra *seen*·go·la single room

camicia ① ka·*mee*·cha shirt

camminare ka·mee·*na*·re walk

campagna ① kam·*pa*·nya countryside

cancellare kan·che·*la*·re cancel

cane ⓜ *ka*·ne dog

cappello ⓜ ka·*pe*·lo hat

cappotto ⓜ ka·*po*·to coat

carabinieri ⓜ pl ka·ra·bee·*nye*·ree police (military)

carne ① *kar*·ne meat

caro/a ⓜ/① *ka*·ro/a expensive

carrozza ① **ristorante** ka·ro·tsa rees·to·*ran*·te dining car

carta ① **d'identità** *kar*·ta dee·den·tee·*ta* identification card (ID)

carta ① **d'imbarco** *kar*·ta deem·*bar*·ko boarding pass

carta ① **di credito** *kar*·ta dee *kre*·dee·to credit card

cartolaio ⓜ kar·to·*la*·yo stationer

cartolina ① kar·to·*lee*·na postcard

cassiere/a ⓜ/① ka·*sye*·re/a cashier

cattivo/a ⓜ/① ka·*tee*·vo/a bad

celibe ⓜ *che*·lee·be single (man)

cellulare ⓜ che·loo·*la*·re mobile phone

cena ① *che*·na dinner

centro ⓜ **commerciale** *chen*·tro ko·mer·*cha*·le shopping centre

cerotti ⓜ pl che·*ro*·tee Band-aids
chi kee who
chiave ⓕ *kya*·ve key
chiuso/a ⓜ/ⓕ *kyoo*·zo/a closed · shut · locked
ciascuno/a ⓜ/ⓕ chas·*koo*·no/a each
cintura ⓕ **di sicurezza** cheen·*too*·ra dee see·koo·*re*·tsa seatbelt
circo ⓜ *cheer*·ko circus
città ⓕ chee·*ta* city
classe ⓕ **business** *kla*·se *beez*·nes business class
classe ⓕ **turistica** *kla*·se too·*ree*·stee·ka economy class
collant ⓜ pl ko·*lant* pantyhose
commedia ⓕ ko·*me*·dya play (theatre)
comodo/a ⓜ/ⓕ *ko*·mo·do/a comfortable
compagno/a ⓜ/ⓕ kom·*pa*·nyo/a companion · partner (intimate)
compleanno ⓜ kom·ple·*a*·no birthday
completo/a ⓜ/ⓕ kom·*ple*·to/a booked out
comprare kom·*pra*·re buy
compreso/a ⓜ/ⓕ kom·*pre*·zo/a included
condividere kon·dee·*vee*·de·re share (with)
confermare kon·fer·*ma*·re confirm (a booking)
confine ⓜ kon·*fee*·ne border
congelato/a ⓜ/ⓕ kon·je·*la*·to/a frozen
conto ⓜ *kon*·to bill (account)
conto ⓜ **in banca** *kon*·to een *ban*·ka bank account
convalidare kon·va·lee·*da*·re validate
coperta ⓕ ko·*per*·ta blanket
coperto ⓜ ko·*per*·to cover charge (restaurant)
cucina ⓕ koo·*chee*·na kitchen
cucinare koo·chee·*na*·re cook
cuoco/a ⓜ/ⓕ *kwo*·ko/a cook · chef (restaurant)

cuoio ⓜ *kwo*·yo leather
cuscino ⓜ koo·*shee*·no pillow

- d -

data ⓕ **di nascita** *da*·ta dee *na*·shee·ta date of birth
deposito ⓜ de·*po*·zee·to deposit (bank)
deposito ⓜ **bagagli** de·*po*·zee·to ba·*ga*·lyee left luggage (office)
diapositiva ⓕ dee·a·po·zee·*tee*·va slide (film)
dimensioni ⓕ pl dee·men·*syo*·nee size (general)
diretto/a ⓜ/ⓕ dee·*re*·to/a direct
distributore ⓜ **automatico di biglietti** dee·stree·boo·*to*·re ow·to·*ma*·tee·ko dee bee·*lye*·tee ticket machine
distributore ⓜ **di servizio** dee·stree·boo·*to*·re ser·*vee*·tsyo petrol station · service station
dito ⓜ *dee*·to finger
doccia ⓕ *do*·cha shower
dogana ⓕ do·*ga*·na customs
domani do·*ma*·nee tomorrow
domani mattina do·*ma*·nee ma·*tee*·na tomorrow morning
domani pomeriggio do·*ma*·nee po·me·*ree*·jo tomorrow afternoon
domani sera do·*ma*·nee *se*·ra tomorrow evening
dopodomani do·po·do·*ma*·nee day after tomorrow
dormire dor·*mee*·re sleep
dove *do*·ve where
drogheria ⓕ dro·ge·*ree*·a grocery

- e -

edicola ⓕ e·*dee*·ko·la newsagency
edificio ⓜ e·dee·*fee*·cho building
elenco ⓜ **telefonico** e·*len*·ko te·le·*fo*·nee·ko phone book
entrare en·*tra*·re enter

entrata ① en·*tra*·ta entry
erba ① *er*·ba grass
esposizione ① es·po·zee·*tsyo*·ne exhibition
espresso/a ⓜ/① es·*pre*·so/a express
est ⓜ est east
estate ① es·*ta*·te summer

~ f ~

fagioli ⓜ pl fa·*jo*·lee beans
famiglia ① fa·*mee*·lya family
fantastico/a ⓜ/① fan·*tas*·tee·ko/a great
farmacia ① far·ma·*chee*·a pharmacy
federa ① *fe*·de·ra pillowcase
figlia ① *fee*·lya daughter
figlio ⓜ *fee*·lyo son
finestra ① fee·*nes*·tra window (general)
finestrino ⓜ fee·nes·*tree*·no window (car, plane)
foresta ① fo·*res*·ta forest
fra poco fra *po*·ko soon
francobollo ⓜ fran·ko·*bo*·lo stamp
fratello ⓜ fra·*te*·lo brother
freno ⓜ *fre*·no brake
fresco/a ⓜ/① *fres*·ko/a fresh
fumare foo·*ma*·re smoke

~ g ~

galleria ① **d'arte** ga·le·*ree*·a *dar*·te art gallery
gentile jen·*tee*·le kind • nice (person)
giacca ① *ja*·ka jacket
giallo/a ⓜ/① *ja*·lo/a yellow
giardino ⓜ jar·*dee*·no garden
gioielli ⓜ pl jo·*ye*·lee jewellery
giornale ⓜ jor·*na*·le newspaper
giorno ⓜ *jor*·no day
gita ① *jee*·ta tour • trip
gonna ① *go*·na skirt
grande *gran*·de big • large

grande magazzino ⓜ *gran*·de ma·ga·*dzee*·no department store
gratuito/a ⓜ/① gra·*too*·ee·to/a free (gratis) • complimentary (free)
grigio/a ⓜ/① *gree*·jo/a grey
gruppo **sanguigno** *groo*·po san·*gwee*·nyo blood group
guanti ⓜ *gwan*·tee gloves
guardaroba ⓜ gwar·da·*ro*·ba cloakroom

~ i ~

ieri *ye*·ree yesterday
in fondo een *fon*·do at the bottom • after all
in lista d'attesa een *lee*·sta da·*te*·za standby (ticket)
in ritardo een ree·*tar*·do late (adv)
incidente ⓜ een·chee·*den*·te accident • crash
influenza ① een·floo·*en*·tsa flu • influenza
informazioni ① pl een·for·ma·*tsyo*·nee information
inglese een·*gle*·ze English
insieme een·*sye*·me together
Internet point ⓜ *een*·ter·net poynt Internet cafe
interprete ⓜ/① een·*ter*·pre·te interpreter
intervallo ⓜ een·ter·*va*·lo intermission
inverno ⓜ een·*ver*·no winter
itinerario ⓜ ee·tee·ne·*ra*·ryo itinerary • route

~ l ~

lana ① *la*·na wool
latte ⓜ *la*·te milk
lavanderia la·van·de·*ree*·a laundry (room)
lavanderia a gettone la·van·de·*ree*·a je·*to*·ne laundrette
lavare la·*va*·re wash (something)
lavarsi la·*var*·see wash (oneself)

lavatrice ① la·va·*tree*·che washing machine
Lei lay you pol
lettera ① *le*·te·ra letter
letto ⑨ *le*·to bed
letto ⑨ **matrimoniale** *le*·to ma·*tree*·mo·*nya*·le double bed
libreria ① lee·bre·*ree*·a bookshop
libretto ⑨ **di circolazione** lee·*bre*·to dee cheer·ko·la·*tsyo*·ne car owner's title
libro ⑨ *lee*·bro book
linea ① **aerea** *lee*·ne·a a·e·*re*·a airline
Loro *lo*·ro you pl pol
luna ① **di miele** *loo*·na dee *mye*·le honeymoon

-m-

macchina ① ma·*kee*·na car · machine
macchina ① **fotografica** ma·*kee*·na fo·to·*gra*·fee·ka camera
macelleria ① ma·che·le·*ree*·a butcher's shop
madre ① *ma*·dre mother
maglione ⑨ ma·*lyo*·ne jumper · sweater
mancia ① *man*·cha tip (gratuity)
mangiare man·*ja*·re eat
marciapiede ⑨ mar·cha·*pye*·de footpath
mare ⑨ *ma*·re sea
marrone ⑨/① ma·*ro*·ne brown
mattina ① ma·*tee*·na morning
medicina ① me·dee·*chee*·na medicine
medico ⑨ me·*dee*·ko doctor
mercato ⑨ mer·*ka*·to market
mese ⑨ *me*·ze month
mezzanotte ① me·dza·*no*·te midnight
mezzo ⑨ *me*·dzo half
moda ① *mo*·da fashion
moglie ① *mo*·lye wife
montagna ① mon·*ta*·nya mountain
mostrare mos·*tra*·re show

multa ① *mool*·ta fine (payment)
musica ① *moo*·zee·ka music

-n-

Natale ⑨ na·*ta*·le Christmas
negozio ⑨ ne·*go*·tsyo shop
nero/a ⑨/① ne·ro/a black
neve ① *ne*·ve snow
no no no
noleggiare no·le·*ja*·re hire
nome ⑨ *no*·me name
non non no · not
non fumatore non foo·ma·*to*·re non-smoking
nord ⑨ nord north
notte ① *no*·te night
nubile ① *noo*·bee·le single (woman)
numero ⑨ *noo*·me·ro number
numero ⑨ **di camera** *noo*·me·ro dee *ka*·me·ra room number
nuotare nwo·*ta*·re swim

-o-

occhiali ⑨ pl o·*kya*·lee glasses (spectacles)
oggi o·*jee* today
olio ⑨ o·*lyo* oil
ora ① o·ra hour
orario ⑨ o·*ra*·ryo timetable
orario ⑨ **di apertura** o·*ra*·ryo dee a·per·*too*·ra opening hours
oro ⑨ o·ro gold
ospedale ⑨ os·pe·*da*·le hospital
ostello ⑨ **della gioventù** os·*te*·lo de·la jo·ven·*too* youth hostel
ovest ⑨ o·vest west

-p-

padre ⑨ *pa*·dre father
pagamento ⑨ pa·ga·*men*·to payment
palazzo ⑨ pa·*la*·tso palace

pane ⓜ *pa*·ne bread
panetteria ⓕ pa·ne·te·*ree*·a bakery
pannolino ⓜ pa·no·*lee*·no diaper •
nappy
pantaloni ⓜ pl pan·ta·*lo*·nee pants •
trousers
parrucchiere ⓜ pa·roo·*kye*·re beauty
salon
partenza ⓕ par·*ten*·tsa departure
partire par·*tee*·re depart • leave
passaporto ⓜ pa·sa·*por*·to
passport
passeggero/a ⓜ/ⓕ pa·se·*je*·ro/a
passenger
passeggiata ⓕ pa·se·*ja*·ta walk
pasticceria ⓕ pa·stee·che·*ree*·a
cake shop
pasto ⓜ *pas*·to meal
patente ⓕ **(di guida)** pa·*ten*·te (dee
gwee·da) drivers licence
pellicola ⓕ pe·*lee*·ko·la film (for
camera)
penna ⓕ **(a sfera)** *pe*·na (a *sfe*·ra)
pen (ballpoint)
pensionato/a ⓜ/ⓕ pen·syo·*na*·to/a
pensioner • retired
perché per·*ke* why • because
perso/a ⓜ/ⓕ *per*·so/a lost
pescheria ⓕ pe·ske·*ree*·a fish shop
pezzo ⓜ **di antiquariato** *pe*·tso dee
an·tee·kwa·*rya*·to antique
piano ⓜ *pya*·no floor (storey)
pila ⓕ *pee*·la battery
piscina ⓕ pee·*shee*·na swimming
pool
pittore/pittrice ⓜ/ⓕ pee·*to*·re/
pee·*tree*·che painter
pittura ⓕ pee·*too*·ra painting (the
art)
polizia ⓕ po·lee·*tsee*·a police
(civilian)
pomeriggio ⓜ po·me·*ree*·jo
afternoon
portacenere ⓜ por·ta·*che*·ne·re
ashtray
portatile ⓜ por·*ta*·tee·le laptop

posta ⓕ *pos*·ta mail
posta ⓕ **ordinaria** *pos*·ta
or·dee·*na*·rya surface mail
posta ⓕ **prioritaria** *pos*·ta
pree·o·ree·*ta*·rya express mail
posteggio ⓜ **di tassì** po·*ste*·jo dee
ta·*see* taxi stand
posto ⓜ **di polizia** *pos*·to dee
po·lee·*tsee*·a police station
pranzo ⓜ *pran*·dzo lunch
prenotare pre·no·*ta*·re book (make
a booking)
preservativo ⓜ pre·zer·va·*tee*·vo
condom
presto ⓜ/ⓕ *pres*·to early
prezzo ⓜ *pre*·tso price
prima classe ⓕ *pree*·ma *kla*·se first
class
prima colazione ⓕ *pree*·ma
ko·la·*tsyo*·ne breakfast
primavera ⓕ pree·ma·*ve*·ra spring
(season)
prossimo/a ⓜ/ⓕ *pro*·see·mo/a next
pulce ⓕ *pool*·che flea
pulito/a ⓜ/ⓕ poo·*lee*·to/a clean
pulizia ⓕ poo·lee·*tsee*·a cleaning
pullman ⓜ *pool*·man bus (coach)

- q -

quadro ⓜ *kwa*·dro painting (canvas)
quando *kwan*·do when
qui *kwee* here

- r -

raccomandata ⓕ ra·ko·man·*da*·ta
registered mail
ragazza ⓕ ra·*ga*·tsa girl(friend)
ragazzo ⓜ ra·*ga*·tso boy(friend)
regalo ⓜ re·*ga*·lo present (gift)
reggiseno ⓜ re·jee·*se*·no bra
registrazione ⓕ re·jee·stra·*tsyo*·ne
check-in (hotel)
resto ⓜ *res*·to change (money)

ricetta ① ree·*che*·ta prescription

ricevuta ① ree·che·*voo*·ta receipt

rimborso ⓜ reem·*bor*·so refund

riparare ree·pa·*ra*·re repair

ritardo ⓜ ree·*tar*·do delay

ritiro ⓜ **bagagli** ree·*tee*·ro ba·ga·lyee baggage claim

ritorno ⓜ ree·*tor*·no return

rosa ① *ro*·za pink

rosso/a ⓜ/① *ro*·so/a red

rubato/a ⓜ/① roo·*ba*·to/a stolen

~ s ~

sacchetto ⓜ sa·*ke*·to bag (shopping)

sacco ⓜ **a pelo** *sa*·ko a *pe*·lo sleeping bag

sala ① **di transito** *sa*·la dee *tran*·zee·to transit lounge

sala ① **d'attesa** *sa*·la da·*te*·za waiting room

salumeria ① sa·loo·me·*ree*·a delicatessen

salva slip ⓜ pl *sal*·va sleep panty liners

sarto/a ⓜ/① *sar*·to/a tailor

scale ① pl *ska*·le stairway

scarpe ① pl *skar*·pe shoes

scatola ① *ska*·to·la box • carton • can • tin

scheda ① **telefonica** *ske*·da te·le·fo·*nee*·ka phone card

schiena ① *skye*·na back (body)

sconto ⓜ *skon*·to discount

secco/a ⓜ/① *se*·ko/a dry

sedile ⓜ se·*dee*·le seat (chair)

seggiovia ① se·jo·*vee*·a chairlift (skiing)

sentiero ⓜ sen·*tye*·ro path • track • trail

senza *sen*·tsa without

servizio ⓜ ser·*vee*·tsyo service • service-charge

settimana ① se·tee·*ma*·na week

sicuro/a ⓜ/① see·*koo*·ro/a safe

sigaretta ① see·ga·*re*·ta cigarette

soccorso ⓜ so·*kor*·so help • aid

soldi ⓜ pl *sol*·dee money • cash

solo andata ① *so*·lo an·*da*·ta one-way

sorella ① so·*re*·la sister

spiaggia ① *spya*·ja beach

sporco/a ⓜ/① *spor*·ko/a dirty

spuntino ⓜ spoon·*tee*·no snack

stagione ① sta·*jo*·ne season

stanza ① *stan*·tsa room

stazione ① **d'autobus** sta·*tsyo*·ne *dow*·to·boos bus station

stazione ① **della metropolitana** sta·*tsyo*·ne de·la me·tro·po·lee·*ta*·na metro station

stazione ① **ferroviaria** sta·*tsyo*·ne fe·ro·*vyar*·ya train station

sterlina ① ster·*lee*·na pound (money)

straniero/a ⓜ/① stra·*nye*·ro/a foreign

studente/studentessa ⓜ/① stoo·*den*·te/stoo·den·*te*·sa student

sud ⓜ sood south

suocera ① *swo*·che·ra mother-in-law

supermercato ⓜ soo·per·mer·*ka*·to supermarket

sveglia ① *sve*·lya alarm clock

~ t ~

tardi *tar*·dee late (adj)

temperino ⓜ tem·pe·*ree*·no penknife

tossire to·*see*·re cough

traghetto ⓜ tra·*ge*·to ferry

trucco ⓜ *troo*·ko make-up

tu too you inf

tutto ⓜ *too*·to everything

~ u ~

ubriaco/a ⓜ/① oo·bree·*a*·ko/a drunk

ufficio ⓜ oo·*fee*·cho office

ufficio ⓜ **del turismo** oo·*fe*[...] too·*reez*·mo tourist office

ufficio ⓜ **oggetti smarriti** oo·*fee*·cho o·*je*·tee sma·*ree*·tee lost property office

ufficio ⓜ **postale** oo·*fee*·cho pos·*ta*·le post office

ultimo/a ⓜ/ⓕ *ool*·tee·mo/a last

uomo ⓜ *wo*·mo man

uscire con oo·*shee*·re kon go out with

uscita ⓕ oo·*shee*·ta exit

~ V ~

vacanze ⓕ pl va·*kan*·tse holidays

vagone ⓜ **letto** va·*go*·ne *le*·to sleeping car

valigetta ⓕ va·lee·*je*·ta briefcase

veloce ve·*lo*·che fast

verde *ver*·de green

verdura ⓕ ver·*doo*·ra vegetable

via ⓕ **aerea** *vee*·a a·e·*re*·a airmail

viaggio ⓜ **d'affari** vee·*a*·jo da·*fa*·ree business trip

videoregistratore ⓜ vee·de·o·re·jee·stra·*to*·re video

vino ⓜ *vee*·no wine

viola vee·o·la purple

visita ⓕ **guidata** vee·zee·ta gwee·*da*·ta guided tour

vista ⓕ *vee*·sta view

vocabolarietto ⓜ vo·ka·bo·la·*rye*·to phrasebook

vocabolario ⓜ vo·ka·bo·*la*·ryo dictionary

volo ⓜ *vo*·lo flight

~ Z ~

zaino ⓜ *dzai*·no backpack • knapsack

zia ⓕ *tsee*·a aunt

Acknowledgments
Associate Product Director Angela Tinson
Product Editor Kathryn Rowan
Language Writers Pietro Iagnocco, Karina Coates, Susie Walker, Mirna Cicioni, Anna Beltrami
Cover Designer Campbell McKenzie

Thanks
Kate Chapman, Gwen Cotter, James Hardy, Indra Kilfoyle, Wibowo Rusli, Juan Winata

Published by Lonely Planet Global Ltd
CRN 554153

4th Edition – June 2018
Text © Lonely Planet 2018
Cover Image Arch of Peace, Milan, Italy – Marco Bottigelli/AWL ©

Printed in China   10 9 8 7 6 5 4

Index

INDEX

10. Phrases to Get You Talking

Hello.	Buongiorno. bwon·*jor*·no
Goodbye.	Arrivederci. a·ree·ve·*der*·chee
Please.	Per favore. per fa·*vo*·re
Thank you.	Grazie. *gra*·tsye
Excuse me.	Mi scusi. mee *skoo*·zee
Sorry.	Mi dispiace. mee dees·*pya*·che
Yes.	Sì. see
No.	No. no
I don't understand.	Non capisco. non ka·*pee*·sko
How much is it?	Quanto costa? *kwan*·to *kos*·ta